FOR MY GOOD
BUT,
FOR HIS GLORY

It's raw, it's real, are you ready for the truth?

Tarrian LaShun Pace

FOR MY GOOD

BUT,

FOR HIS GLORY

it's raw, It's real, are you ready for the truth?

For My Good, But For His Glory
by Tarrian LaShun Pace

Printed in the United States of America

ISBN 1-591607-44-2

Unless otherwise indicated, Bible quotations are taken from the Children of Color Holy Bible, King James Version, Copyright © 1997 by World Publishing, Inc., and the Amplified Bible/ Zondervan, Copyright © 1987 by The Zondervan Corporation and the Lockman Foundation.

Table of Contents

The Introduction

If any man have an ear let him hear. [Rev. 13:9]

Blessed is he that readeth, and they that hear... and keep those things which are written therein. [Rev. 1:3]

I am Alpha and Omega, the beginning and the ending, saith the Lord, which is, and which was, and which is to come, the Almighty. [Rev. 1:8]

PRESENTATION

This Book is presented

To _____

From _____

This day of _____

Year of our Lord _____

Opening Prayer

PLEASE, before you read this book, say this prayer:

Father, you said that if I confess with my mouth the Lord Jesus and believe with my heart that God, raised Christ from the dead, I will be saved. For with my heart I believe your righteousness and with my mouth I confess salvation. Lord forgive me of all my sins: every kind and all types of sin, wash me in your blood Lord Jesus and make me completely whole. I accept you into my life as my Lord, Saviour and Master. Father now fill me with your precious Spirit, the Holy Ghost, in Jesus name I pray, Amen.

And It Is So!

Prophecy Fulfilled

Oh that my words
Were now written!
Oh that they were
Printed in a book.

Job 19:23

Dedication I

To

Xenia

This book is dedicated to you,
My heart is now short of a beat
Because that one, belonged to you.

And we release you into the hands of a God,
who did not make a mistake.
Dr. Marlene (Mom) Tally
Philadelphia, PA.

Dedication II

This book is dedicated to the woman who has at one time let God down or felt she let herself down, but did not permit the negative circumstances or mistakes of her life rehearse her future. But with impregnable determination, to become the woman of God he predestined you to be.

From the Author

Dear Sisters and Brothers, upon the command of the Lord was this book written. Not that I've gone through something so special or worse than anybody else, but I have allowed the Lord to take my life and these experiences of my life, to be used for his glory, not knowing all the time that it would work out for my good. To my brothers, please! Know that I'm not male bashing men, for I am thankful to God for his illimitable sagacity in ordaining the male for us females.

For the husbands who may be reading this book, concerning your wives, you should love them, honor them, and respect them. For the word of the Lord says for you to dwell with her according to knowledge, (God's knowledge) and honor her as the weaker vessel… that your prayers won't be hindered. [I Peter,3:7]

And for the single brothers who may be reading this book, don't play with a woman's emotions or her love, you know the very first time you see a woman if she's your type or kind, you know what you want in a woman for a wife. So if she doesn't fit your standards, leave her alone. And don't ask for the prize before the race, and if you're burning, the bible says to marry, not shack. If you are the bee for her then don't just taste the honey, buy the hive, and the comb will belong to you.

For the wives who may be reading this book, the word of the

Lord says for you to obey, love, honor, respect, and be in subjection to your own husband. Because he is the head of you and Christ is the head of him, and the head of Christ is God. [I Cor. 11:3] I believe there would be fewer divorces, negative lifestyles and situations if men and women would give their lives to God and take their rightful place in the home and in society.

And for the single sisters who may be reading this book, you are to stay busy working for the Lord and yourself, until God sends that elect, valuable, and absolute person into your life. Sisters don't play with a man's emotions, or love, you know the first time you see him if you like him or not. If you're not interested then don't lead him on.

If you play with fire, you will get burned. Can a man take fire into his bosom…and not be burned? [Prov.6:27]

Husbands, wives, men, and women, what we need is a faithful prayer life which will give us a relationship with God. And if we are faithful to God, then we can be faithful to each other. If there's a problem in your marriage, go to God who knows each of us individually asking him what can we do to make things right and each other happy.

And for the singles who are in relationships and things are going wrong, go to God asking him if this person is really the one he wants you to have as a spouse. This is a life time commitment, you should not enter into it lightly, think before you wreck your life, her life and the lives of the children you may have and the families involved. We are all humans with feelings, so let's handle each other with prayer and tender loving Jesus care.

So as you prayerfully read this book, please know I'm not trying to hurt anyone, just a servant of the Lord, his handmaiden, anointed to do a special work, wanting to help someone not make the same mistakes I did. The truth is revealed, God said for me to spare nothing, for it is the truth that sets us free, today I am free, not because I wrote this book, for he made me free before. And for this reason I was able to do this book, my pain for his gain. The God of Abraham, Issac, Jacob, and LaShun Pace.

Servant of the Most High God.

Author's Prayer

Father in the name of your son Jesus,
I bear my soul in this book that millions
Of other souls may come to you for
Salvation
Healing
Refuge
And
Deliverance.

It is to you I dedicate this book, for your glory.

Thank you I

I would like to thank: My heavenly Father, Jesus Christ my Lord and Saviour and the Holy Ghost my best friend. My parents, Supt. Murphy Pace Jr. and Missy. Bettie Ann Pace for raising me up in the fear of God and teaching me how to pray and seek God for myself. My brother, M.J. Pace I love you, thanks for all you've done for me and been to me. My sisters, who are the jewels in my crown. Duranice (my girlfriend/movie partner). Phyllis (the mother of our children, thanks for just being there through it all). June (my First Lady/friend, love ya much). Melonda (the one I look up to, I admire your strength). DeJuaii (thanks for your strong quiet support). Leslie (our Mother in Zion, keep running). Latrice Pace Speights (thanks for taking care of me out on the road, it takes someone special to take a back seat and serve, I will never forget you). Lydia (our prayer warrior/comedian). My brother, friend and Pastor, Dennis L. Martin Sr. thanks for being there all the time. My brother Micah Speights, love your ability and ideas of music, you're God's best, love ya. Liza Pace, my friend/movie partner, thanks for all your help, prayers, and advice. Vernon Jones my brother/ number one fan, I love you very much. To my god parents, Prophet Floyd and Bertha Brown. Bishop G.E. and Louise Patterson. Bishop Kenneth Bacon. To all my spiritual moms and dads. My god children, Alencia Lewis, Cameron Maxwell, Terrion Andrews,

Nicholas Andrews, Jada MyAngel Haddock. To my church family, Holy Trinity C.O.G.I.C. Lena Martin, D.L. Martin, Demarcus Love, Diamond Pace, Tony Pace, Blake Wesley Pace, Unique, my adopted sisters, Catherine Middelton, Donna Cook, Sabrina Allen, Alexis. To my aces in Texas, Tarsha Jackson, Kristie Patton. To my best girlfriends, Ivy McGregor, and Minister Claudalle Camp, thanks for helping me see this book through to the end. My M.D. Brian Andrews thanks for being there. To all those who prayed for me. My Lawyer, Vincent L. Dimmock. JLM productions. My uncle, Curtis Eugene Martin, thanks for teaching me all about life on the evangelistic field, love you always. Xulon Press. Last but not least, my "left baby" Aarion M. Rhodes, my strength and my joy, I thank God he left me with one, mama loves her baby! You hold a place and space in my heart no one else can ever take. Thanks to all.

Thank You II

To the men God allowed to pass through my life,
I dedicate this book to you as well, thank you for
Every experience, how do I see them?

Blind,
Slippery hands,
No balls and
Small pockets.

You never knew who I was,
therefore you could have never loved me.

Your lost
My hurt
God's gain.

CHAPTER ONE

But it happened to me

But it happened to me

C ome, let me talk with you for awhile so that you may know that the very thing you are going through, is for your good, and for God's glory. How do I know? It happened to me.

It was only two months after our marriage vows, it seems as though I can hear the phone ringing, when my love answered the phone and on the other end was "doctor Aids." I knew something was wrong from the quietness that came from him, but I acted as if nothing was going on, we'd just finished up dinner for the evening and I was doing the normal chores of cleaning when he said, honey; the phone is for you. I said hello, and the doctor asked if my love had talked to me, I asked concerning what? He went on to say that they had found the virus which causes aids in my loves body and that I needed to get to his office right away for testing. The phone call was to make sure that I knew what was going on and if I didn't, he was going to send someone out to the house to tell me. He finished telling me of the danger I was in and that the end results would be death and having children would be no possibility. I gave the phone back to my love, he hung up, we sat on the loveseat, which was all we had besides a component set to play music on, a dining room table and a mattress set in our bed room. Sitting there not knowing that the next words from him would devastate and change my entire life. He told me about the virus, I burst into tears, and the thought of us both dying was too much to bear. Questions were filling my head, all I could say was, I've just gotten married! What is going on? This was back in 1986, I had heard of the alternative life styles of other people but I didn't know about the disease that came from the very act.

Afterwards I left him sitting there and went into the bedroom, fell across the bed crying, and started talking to God. I prayed Lord! If you gave me this man (as I thought he did) for my husband, then I'm asking for a miracle. After I'd talked to God I knew he had heard my prayer. My brother and Pastor at that time, M.J. Pace had announced an up coming revival with our state bishop, well one night during service, the bishop was taking the offering, I was the first to get in line, while standing there, the bishop said, God just spoke and said; someone is going to receive healing in this line tonight. Needless to say I started spinning like a whirlwind saying thank you Jesus! Mind you I had not told a soul.

Going back to the day I got the news from the doctor, my sisters and I had a rehearsal, after arriving at church, walking down the center isle, the organist was playing, and then he stopped, looked at me and said, the Lord just told me to tell you he has put healing in your hands. Again I had not told anything to anybody, but God. Let's go back a few more years, when my family doctor said congratulations Mr. and Mrs. Pace, it's another girl. Before me there were four, one boy, and three girls. After me there came five more girls, my daddy wanted a famous "star baseball team" all Paces; nine boys and one girl, he got just the opposite, a group of preachers and singers. Growing up in a three bedroom house in a subdivision called "Poole Creek" we had so much fun there, playing baseball in the street until the sun went down, my mother's rule were, when the street lights came on, we were to come into the house or we would get it, and we all know what "it" was. There were many rules she had, and we obeyed all of them or we got, (yea you know) "It."

My mother was and yet remains a praying woman, back then when I was a little girl, she'd pick us up from school around twelve noon and head straight to that old tent service, out by the fair grounds. We would hear good preaching and great singing that would rock our heart and soul. We did this every summer until I was about twelve. I watched my mother endure some hurting things from so called church folks, people in the neighborhood, dealing with us girls, and my brother who wanted to be a pimp in a pink Cadillac. But I saw how God moved through her crying out and praying to him. She was a strict disciplinarian, after prayer time, which we always participated in, another rule, she heard us singing the (C.O.G.I.C.) church of God in Christ, yes Lord Praise, when the Lord told her to start gathering us together to sing, and so she did. We would be in the kitchen banging on pots and pans and singing, my daddy was a quartet singer traveling every where, and on Wednesday nights they would rehearse. I'd stay up listening, until my mother made me go to bed. I love my mother, but I was a daddy's girl, I love, love, love my daddy, if I could be with him every where he went, I was there, my mother taught us to serve him first at all meal times, and in-between times, why? Because he was our daddy, the provider of the family, so we didn't mind doing for him because we loved him, and we did the same towards our brother.

We were taught to honor the men of the family as the head of the household, just as the bible teaches, but little do men know, that the smallest thing they do to hurt us goes deeper than they could ever imagine.

My daddy was a carpenter, anything with wood he could make. He did work for big companies and built cabinets for lots of homes, no matter where he had to go for his deliveries, after he'd put the finishing touches on his work, I'd be right there with him, some-times in my bed clothes if it was late. I just wanted to be with him, watching him work, admiring him as my daddy, a strong black man (smile). What I saw in him was what I wanted to marry when I got old enough to do so.

One night while working with my Dad, I did something wrong and he called me a name, "gunk" whatever that was, all I know it made me feel like nothing, worthless, and any other feelings you may think of, that's how I felt. I ran out the door, into the house, not stopping until I got to my bed crying myself to sleep. Now looking back, he never realized how he'd hurt me using those kinds of words. Meanwhile back at the Creek, having the love and admiration for my daddy, the blow of his words hit me harder than I thought, O by the way we haven't been properly introduced; Hi my name is Tarrian LaShun Pace. I'm the fifth child and the fourth daughter, out of ten, yep, the middle child, the one always trying too hard, trying to fit in, wanting to be accepted, wanting every one to love me, not wanting to hurt a soul, very low self esteem, never thought I was pretty, wanting to belong, but to no avail. This was a recurring event at home, church, school, work, where ever, so I got hurt a lot, more times I care to remember. So growing up looking for the love of my daddy and wanting the acceptance of others threw me in a cycle of bad relationships, marriage and divorce. (Excuse me; I keep getting ahead of myself) In this three bedroom house, my brother had his room, my parents, of course had theirs and being much smaller than we are now all nine girls slept in two full size beds, but when we got older my daddy built us beds in the wall like army bunks, four on each side walls and two in the middle under the window, by day the top middle bunk was a desk and at night it was a bed, there was another C shape desk in the left corner of the room. We all shared one closet, can you imagine the clothes? My mother bought two large three feet barrels so that we would have space for extra clothes, because the one, four feet long pole just wasn't enough. Wash day, O how I wished I could disappear, clothes would be tall as the pile of leaves outside during the fall, one day the washing machine broke down, we had about four large yard bags filled with clothes and after washing, if mother didn't have enough coins to dry, we would come home and spread them on the clothes lines, the bushes and the neighbor's lines, so at the end of the day we'd all split up going around the neighborhood gathering up clothes.

But after a long hard day of working, washing, folding and putting clothes away, my mother would be preparing a wonderful dinner for us, which was what ever we could afford at that time after daddy finished paying bills, we were in the som-por-not class; we weren't poor and we weren't middle class or rich. I know you want to know what is "som-por-not", it is sometimes "poor" and sometimes "not" what ever we were, it didn't matter because of the love, the joy, and the good times we would have not just at home but with children in the neighborhood.

But out of all my sisters I was the tomboy of the crew I could climb a tree faster than anybody in the hood, run faster and throw a pretty good ball, I loved nature and still do, I wanted to be a professional photographer but my dad could not afford to pay for the photography classes at school, so I threw that dream out of the window, it may come around again. We sang at the P.T.A. meetings which I hated with a passion, because it seemed like after every P.T.A. I got a whipping, I didn't understand. I was a good little girl, but my mouth would get me in trouble sometimes, and hanging with the wrong girls at school trying to fit in. One day the teacher said to me Pace, I'm surprised at you behaving the way you are, I said back to her, I'm surprised at you; that was one of the worse beatings I ever got in my life; another time I was outside fighting or should I say trying to fight, because I could not fight, but I had a mean swing, ya'll know what I'm talking bout (smile) I was out there swinging when my mother pulled up in the car, she didn't even say a word to me, she didn't even ask what happened or how it got started, all she knew was my child is out here fighting and she know what I've taught them, my mother didn't believe in fighting, but my daddy on the other hand did; so what's a child to do? Sometimes you just don't care, you just go for it, so I went for it and I got "IT" (smile). It's something how a mother can scold you one minute and the next make you feel like you never did anything wrong, O the power of a mother's love. My mom could cook, even through the week it seemed like Sunday dinner. My mother would run my dad's bath water, clean his ears, wash his feet, cook his favorite meals; she had this wonderful secret steak sauce that she'd make for his steaks (wouldn't you like to know?) (smile); not just wanting a man like my daddy, I also wanted to love a man like my mother yet love my daddy today.

Well I'm a bit older now, fifteen, and traveling is in my future, my uncle has these revivals called camp meetings every summer and winter, guest would come from all across the U.S. to be in the meetings, which is where I met two guys I liked, one was from the north and the other one from the mid west, the mid west guy was the first one I started talking to, he was so fine, tall, built, nice afro, pretty smile and everything, of course I would only see him twice, maybe three times a year if my uncle went to the mid west to his church to preach and we'd go, but whenever I'd see him, I would sing my best, try to look my best, put my legs out and cross them at the ankles, because I thought I had pretty legs plus, I thought all this stuff would get his attention; my beautiful voice, surely when he heard me sing his heart would melt, and in my dress with my small waist and big hips, O I got him for sure, on one event the camp meeting choir which I was a member of went out of town to sing and he was there, but instead of leaving with my sisters, I decided to stay with the choir and sing, because the choir director said he needed me to lead a particular song Saturday night, so I stayed. After we sang we went to some ones, house to eat, the house was filled with people, and I was eating fish with hot sauce, he came over to talk with me asking how was I doing and that he had enjoyed my singing, O I was hooked; we started talking about my mother and I've always said if a man loves my mother he's alright with me, he was saying how cute she was, I didn't like him calling my mother cute, because some where down inside of me, made me think he could like my mother. We exchanged addresses, and the relationship began, so I thought. We started writing each other and girl I just knew this was it, but as time went on I was doing all the writing, with him writing sometimes. I'm a preacher and I travel all the time was the excuse he gave for not writing as often, and I bit the bait. But then he stopped all together with the writing and coming to the camp meetings. Then one camp meeting, I'll never forget; my uncle gave space for a guest minister to give remarks before service ended, and this man was a friend of Mr. Mid West, well the minister was making his closing remarks when

he said, oh I forgot, how many of ya'll know Mr. Mid West? almost every one raised their hands because he was a popular guy, then he went on to say, he got married, sitting on the front row of the church, I wanted to run up the middle isle through the double doors into the street and get hit by a car, but I just sat there motion-less, my friends was like oh no! There was this guy there who was in love with me, but I couldn't stand him, boy when he heard that, he jumped straight up in the air and yelled woo! With this big smile on his face, he told me that I was his wife and now that Mr. Mid West is married, he just knew that I was all his; but I didn't marry him either.

I needed time to heal, yet having to travel and even to the state where he lived not knowing whether I would see him or not, but in the process of time sorry to say, he had divorced, and moved to my city, wouldn't you know it, he came to visit at one of our church services, after church we talked: he had a trip to take about four hours away, he asked if I would ride with him, I said yes, while riding, I began to tell him about how I had feelings for him and how he hurt me when he got married, I told him that I thought he was a church player, he smiled, we laughed, he apologized, of course I forgave him, he said that he didn't know I felt that way about him, I told him it didn't matter and that he was out of my system. We had a nice ride all the way back home, now I never see him anymore, although I wonder how he's doing.

After getting him up and out, in comes another one. Mr. North, Mr. North was tall, slim, nice hair, and a hard worker, in the church and out, not a church player, he really loved the lord, his pastor, and his mother, I was told anytime a man love his mother he will love you, needless to say I started talking to Mr. North, we met at the camp meeting as well, I had been seeing him, but now I saw him. We started writing each other, he'd write and send cards, a very poetic man with passion in his words, a neat dresser always together, nothing out of place, from his home, his car, even the folding of his money, every fold had a crease just perfect, he was a nice guy. We talked for about two years, then the communication between us just stopped and I wasn't trying to see what had happened, so I got married.

Back to February fifteenth, on top of having to deal with the news from the doctor and trying to adjust, my love's sister called saying that she needed to talk to him, she came in, my love was in the shower, I was lying on the bed, she walked right by me, went into the bathroom where he was, without speaking, I was hot. I heard some of the conversation, the door wasn't closed all the way, apparently having problems with the girls she was with, she wanted to move back with her brother. My mother questioned him about her being there and asked if she would be there after we got married, he told her no mam, but, yes mam, there she was back with him and me and that's how it was, him, her and me. We were just newlyweds, it wasn't four months and we had a baby, and not one I had given birth to. I admit, I brought everything upon myself from marrying him, to saying yes to her moving back in with us. People told my parents that I shouldn't marry him because of things they saw, heard and things the lord told them, but did I listen? No, I was tried of being alone, everybody else was getting married or had some one to love but me, plus I wanted to get out of the house and have my own.

How We Met

He was the manager for a world renowned gospel singer who wanted me to be in his group. The Churches of God In Christ were having a convention in Atlanta, and the late night musicals would be at my church, at one of those midnight services my sisters and I had to sing, I was already upset because I didn't have on what I wanted to wear, I had on a blue jean rap around skirt, a colorful striped top blue, brown and a pale yellow, all while we were singing I had an attitude, after we finished I went to my seat, sitting there with my hands folded in my lap, I noticed that someone was looking at me, it was him (my love), he asked me if I was alright, I said NO! rolled my eyes turned my head straight back into the position I was in, after church, standing on the steps, he came out and started talking about nothing, he asked why was I so mad? I told him then he said well, I think you look nice. I said to myself lies, because I had just come from work, cleaning classrooms, it was my mother's job but she'd gotten sick, and I went to work in her stead for three years. I gave her the pay check every payday. I will do anything to help my mother, my daddy or anybody else. Anyway I knew I didn't look good like he was trying to make me believe. I told him bye and continued down the steps when he said wait! The guy I'm managing wants you to be in his group, so I gave him my number, the next week he called to see if I could make it to rehearsal, of course I had to ask my parents, another rule, we had to ask could we go and let them know when we were coming home, I could drive, but I didn't have a car, so I told him yes I could go but I needed a ride, he offered to pick me up but little did he know I wouldn't be alone, another rule, which was two had to go on a date not one. My mother had a saying when we would ask why we couldn't ever go alone, she would say, it's not that I don't trust you baby, I just don't trust the devil.

He picked us up for rehearsal and brought us back, he called again, this time it wasn't a rehearsal night, I asked him why was he calling, he said he just wanted to get to know me better, so we talked very briefly, then the calls started getting more frequent and my mother wanted to know, why was he calling so much? I said, I didn't know, I guest he likes me, then he started coming over, one day he came over with some chicken, we went out on the grass, he had a blanket and all, I said to myself, self he likes you; I said he's alright with me. So we ate and he went home. My mother wanted to know, what was all that about? I said, he said that he was at home thinking about me and that it would be a good day for a pick nick on the grass, she said alright Pick Nick! All he wants to do is pick you now and nick you later. I just laughed and walked on to the bedroom. We began to date on and off. I can remember on one of our dates, my mother gave me some money. I asked her, what is this for, she said, "just in case he starts acting up, you and your sister can catch a cab and come home". I said, "Mother you are something else," she looked at me and said, "I'm serious." About a year later, he gave me an engagement ring without asking my daddy, boy was he hot. But I kept the ring. The talk continued about him, one day in church a mother got up to give her testimony and instead of testifying she started talking about me being engaged; she said, "saints, we need to pray, because the devil is trying to take one of our first family members out of here, pray saints pray!" I just looked at her and began to laugh within.

While laying on the bed sleep one day, something woke me up; mind you I had asked the Lord if we were to marry, it was like the ring got very hot, so hot that it woke me up. It felt like it was burning. I snatched it of so quickly, it went flying across the room. But needless to say, I overlooked the sign: God was trying to tell me something. Months later I gave the ring back and called it off. I was confused, I thought I loved him or did I. I really didn't know. Time went on we started talking again, but this time there was no ring. He has taken it back. At this point I didn't mind because by now I thought I had heard from God myself and that he had told me this man was my husband. No one was saying much because of my attitude, which I could not see at the time, plus he was in my ear. One day he called me, we began to talk and he shared some things with me, like when he was a little boy, he was taken advantage of by a friend of the family. I said, "Okay." But after the conversation I sat there wondering how someone could take advantage of a child like that.

Time went on and it was camp meeting time again. December the twenty seventh, we had just come from church. We all went to the meeting together, but I rode back with him. We got there before everyone else. We parked under the car porch, while waiting on my parents to get home. He asked me would I marry him. With no hesitation, I said, "yes." No thinking about nothing, I just said yes. Then he said, "How are you going to tell your parents? I looked at him and said, "That's your job." By this time my parents were pulling up. I said, "Okay, here they are," he was scared. We got out of the car, then my parents got out of their car, and thus the conversation began. He said, "uh, Daddy Pace, I proposed to Shun and we want to know if it's alright," my daddy didn't give him a chance to finish, he just flew off the handle saying, "well it looks like ya'll have already decided, so you don't need to talk to me," as he went on into the house with my mother following. Things weren't the same any more around the house; yes we spoke to each other, said good morning and all that good stuff. But you could tell that there was, "the marriage thing" in the way. After awhile, my mother gave us a clearance. I began planning for that big day, my wedding. Oh that sounded so good to me, "My Wedding," but we had to pay for every thing, my parents were just there. But, if I had it to do all over again, I would do it the same way, because I would be in the same frame of mind. I know you thought that I was going to say, I would do it differently, but when you are immature in your thinking, no matter how many times you may go through a thing. Until your mind and your thinking mature, you will forever make the same mistakes. Too bad, I didn't know this then (smile). But like the song says, "If I knew back then, what I know now."

THE WEDDING DAY

Now looking back over my life, I wished somebody would have thrown a sheet over my head, threw me in a car, and took off on a long ride to any where. As I was looking at wedding pictures, all the guys looked a little soft, if I may say it that way. They say that love is blind, but wanting to be free and grown so fast can also make you blind. Out of all the praying I was doing, even sometimes fasting, long before I met the man I married, I would say, "Lord, please don't let me grow up and be like Mrs. So and so," and "Lord I don't want to marry a man like Mr. so and so." Yet and still out of all that, "It happened to me."

The wedding was very nice, so I thought. It was at a very prominent black Baptist church, which held about fifteen hundred people, and at least a thousand people were there, we received about three hundred gifts, but none were from my registry. (How you figure?) well maybe one. When the preacher said, "Who give this bride to wed?" my daddy said, "I do," but when the groom came down to get me, my daddy would not turn me loose right away, I felt them tugging, one pulling to the right and the other to the left. Now that I think about it, he was my first real boy friend. He took me on a date, by my self to six flags, and never kissed except on the lips. Even when the preacher said, "you may now salute the bride," he just kissed me on the lips, the audience went, "ah, no", as if to say, "man you can do better than that," maybe these were the things that was going on in my daddy's head, O yea, and the small little detail I left out. I was twenty five years old, and yet a virgin, and my daddy knew that this guy could not even began to appreciate that factor.

THE HONEYMOON

When we got home people were every where, helping put away gifts in our new apartment, doing this, that and the other. So by the time they all left, we went to bed and he said to me, "honey, I'm too pooped to do anything," I said, "Okay," so NOTHING Happened: and when it did, which was the next night, I was in so much pain and I said to myself, if this is what love making is all about? Then they can have it. The next day after we were married, we were at church. Well, I got the moon, now I'm just waiting on the honey. (Smile),

In April, we went to a well known family music convention, and he told me that this trip would be our honeymoon. That year the convention was in Houston, Texas. I really enjoyed the convention, that's all I'm going to say on that. It was after we returned home from our trip, that his sister moved in with us. It wasn't that we didn't like each other or any thing like that. It was just that we were different. We were raised differently, they did things one way and I did them another way. Like every morning she got up to iron her clothes, afterwards she would leave the iron on the kitchen counter. Back then I would hold things in until I was sick and tired, and when I let go, I would hurt some one's feeling, which I didn't like to do. One day I said something to her about leaving the iron on the counter, her response was, "that's what we do at home," I said to my self, "you ain't home." So much for my freedom. Then there was an issue with the car. She worked and I didn't, she had first choice to use it. So there were times I was at home just me, the four walls, the love seat, the mattress set, the television and something to play our music on. Sometimes, I would call my sisters to come and pick me up and wouldn't return until I got good and ready, yea I know it wasn't right but, I did it anyway. I felt like I had the right to do what I did; because he wasn't doing the things a husband was suppose to do. Like giving me money to shop with, knowing that I needed clothes to perform in, and for church, especially when I was making the money too. He would never let me use the ATM card.

Once a friend (soul) saw me at church and noticed that I need some better personal items as a lady, he told his sister to take me to the store and get me what I needed. But for the most part, I did what I was suppose to, like having his dinner ready when he got home form work, I even tried running the bath water thang, washing his feet, and cleaning his ears, trying to be my mother and couldn't, but I deserved an "A" for effort.

I remember one time I had cooked dinner, he and his sister came home together she had the car, so she picked him up from work, when she saw what I had cooked, she didn't want it, so she went into the freezer, took out something else, cooked it and the both of them ate what she cooked. Oh yes, I was upset. Like the old saying goes, two queens can't sit on one throne. So, I began to have talks with my lover, talk after talk, after talk, until he told me she was not leaving. What was I to do? I thought to myself, leave and let her be his wife, but in my mind I said, "Girl things are not looking good here." So yet trying to be a good little house wife, I continued with my daily chores, cooking, cleaning dishes, washing clothes, I would even wax the bathroom floors after I had cleaned it, fold all his under shorts neatly in a draw, all his winter sweaters would be folded neatly on the top of the closet shelf, floors vacuumed, everything was clean, because that's how my mother taught me. I knew how to lay tile on my floors if I didn't like what was down there, put paneling on the walls or put up wall paper, my mother learned from my daddy and she taught it to us. From changing locks to changing diapers we could do mostly anything. But I got tired of him coming home messing up what I had cleaned up. If he wanted a sweater, he would pick one from the middle and all the others would fall to the floor, the same with the under shorts. A woman can only take so much, hangers left on the table after they would iron, dishes left in the sink after I had washed them. Now if it was just the two of us, then I would wink at it a little and even with two you still get tired. But when you have to put up with some one you're not married to, then that's another story. At one time I had taken all I could and I left for about a week and went back home, honestly you should never go back home, but it's good to know that you can. The first reason you shouldn't go back is, it's a major step towards divorce, and it's a type of separation and any type or any kind of separation in a marriage is bad. Even if it's sleeping in the same room, but in separate beds, or different spaces, you're in one room and he's in another, that's a Big NO! NO! Please take it from me, I've been there and done that.

And if you're lying next to your spouse and you can't stand to look at him or the question come in your head why did I marry this person? Or what in the world have I done? Your marriage is in trouble. First, you need to pray together, communicate to and with each other, seek Godly counsel from someone you trust. I did none of these things except for counseling form my Pastor who did not do counseling, only his associate ministers, none of whom I trusted.

My love was troubled too, I latter found out that while an out of town preacher was in town, he went and told him everything we were going through and that I had went back home. The revivalist told him to let me stay at my mother's if that's where I wanted to be. When I heard what the person said, I understood why, they were friends of his. Anyway, I came back home and his sister eventually moved out and things were back to normal again, so I thought. One day we got into an argument about each others family, and he threw up in my face that I forced his sister to move out with all my complaining. He said, I made her feel like she was in a prison, oh boy did he lay a guilt trip on me, I just wanted to die. Me being the kind of person who always wanted everybody to like me, and if they didn't I thought that something was wrong with me. Anyway the argument was about his mother pinching me every time we would go down south to visit and her making me feel like yuck, concerning being her son's wife. I felt like the stupid little house wife who just didn't know anything. But, one day I didn't care what she thought, I called her aside to have a heart to heart, woman to woman talk about her pinching me, I said to her, "now if I pinched you back you would tell my mother that I was disrespecting you, now I'm asking you for the last time, Please! Stop pinching me." She said to me, "that, that was one of her ways she showed affection," I said to her, "well I don't need that kind of affection." Then I said to myself, "I don't see her pinching her children," then she put it on the children she use to teach, saying, that's how she did them, showing her affection, and I said, "well, I'm not one of your students," then I told her, "If there was anything that she needed to tell me that she could come to me and not to her son." I said to her, "we are two grown women, we should be able to talk to each other." After that conversation things were better, but when your husband blames you for things going wrong between his family and you, that's a lot for one person to take, especially when you've tried so hard to make peace.

One day I was just so tired and fed up, I felt trapped like I had no way out, I went and got a razor blade and sat on the bed, tears streaming down my cheeks, I started to make cuts on my wrist, just a little bit of blood was beginning to run, when I heard a knock at the door, I knew it wasn't my love, because he was at work. So I went to the door and to my surprise it was my sister Phyllis and my brother Dennis, who is now my Pastor, he married my sister June. Anyway, I opened the door crying, saying I can't take it any more. They begin to pray immediately, binding the devil and the spirit of suicide, afterwards, I asked what brought them over. Phyllis said that the Lord told her to go to Shun's house. I'm glad she obeyed the voice of God. I really didn't want to die, but I felt hopeless. They stayed for a while and I felt better after they prayed.

We moved from the two bedroom apartment to a studio apartment, because he said that his sister wasn't there to help with the bills and my concert dates wasn't coming in quick enough. But, what I can't understand is when he came to me saying that the Lord told him to quit his job, and to travel with me full time on the road with me, where was the logic in this? But being raised the way I was, if you said, "the Lord said," I listened. So we stayed in the studio apartment for a year. Then one day I went to visit my grandparents and I didn't like what I saw, so I asked my lover if we could move in with them. This way we could save money, and take care of them; so we did.

It's almost three years into our marriage, and living with my grandparents was truly a learning experience for me (God rest their souls). I had to learn how to prepare biscuits from scratch, I remember cooking breakfast for them the very first time, everything smelt good, and looked good to me, I thought, cheese & eggs, bacon, sausage, grits(not instant), apple jelly and can biscuits. Child, I gave them their breakfast, made sure they had everything they needed before we left. My grandmother was just singing my praises about how everything looked so good and smelled good, I felt good about myself, so we left. But when we got back, I was walking down the hallway towards their room when I saw biscuits on the floor in the hall. I said, "Granny, how did these biscuits get in the hallway?" she said to me, "that girl threw them thangs out there," I said, "um, um you are the girl," she just laughed while clapping her hands with her eyes squinted.

As time went on my grandmother began to get tired of being taken care of, this strong black woman, head of the mother's board at church, now helpless and needed everything done for her, and this was not setting well with her at all. At times when I went to bathe her she would be crying, I would have warned her from the other room that I was getting ready to come in and give her a bath for the day. So when I went in she would yell at me telling me to get out, sometimes she would say to me, "I'll do it myself honey," my feelings would be hurt, but I understood, plus she was my elder and I had to obey her. But I would call my daddy, her only son and he would tell her to let me give her a bath and she would. My grandmother and I had some good conversations, she was so funny. I remember one day talking to her, trying to get her to stop dipping snuff. She never believed in doing things like that, but somebody told her that it was good for her and she started taking it, anyway one of the church mothers, her girl friend; had went on to be with the Lord, we took granny to the funeral service and the whole nine yards, I saw the hurt and pain in her eyes as she viewed the body of her friend (Precious). So with all of this in my mind, I thought I would use a little mind psychology on her, so one day while she was sitting on the bed, looking down at her while she was dipping her snuff, I said to her, "grandma, now what if Precious was here to day and she saw you, the church mother dipping snuff, what would she say?" She jerked her body in a backward motion and said to me, "Precious! Precious! Um child we buried her yesterday." I burst out laughing and so did she; I had to leave the room it was over. To this day I still laugh about that. One night as I was walking, the floor would make this squeaking noise, so I heard my grandmother shout, "get out of her," while banging on the side of the bed with this stick she kept, it scared me a little, cause I didn't know what she was doing, so I asked, "grandma, what's the matter? It's just me Shun, going to the bathroom," she then gave a sigh of relief and said, "honey, I was fixing to say that's a mighty big rat." Another night, I had gotten her ready for bed, around seven o'clock, while helping her get under the covers, my lover came in to kiss me good-bye as he went off to work. When he left the room she said to me, again with her eyes closed, "yea, you think he's going to work," I said, "yes he is granny," she didn't respond to me at all. I don't care how old they may get, they know some things we don't. The next morning we cooked breakfast for them, but this time I got on my knees to ask the Lord to teach me and help me to make biscuits the way she use to make them.

I knew all of the ingredients that went into making biscuits, because I had seen my mother and my grandmothers make them, long story short, the Lord helped me and the spirit of my grand-mother fell on me. Needless to say no one can cook home made biscuits like me, nor soul food, but don't ask me because that was then. I don't cook much these days. After we had finished serving them, my lover and I was standing at the sink cleaning up the dishes, when my grandmother said, "Ya'll little girl is gonna have some big legs, because both of ya'll have big legs. I looked at my grandma like why are you staring at our legs, and children, I wasn't thinking about that then, so me and my love looked at each other and laughed. But, little did we know that I was with child that very moment. Three months later I took a pregnancy test and it read positive, went to the doctor, and took another test and he said congratulations, you are about eight weeks into your pregnancy. I was so glad and filled with joy, because the doctor had told us we could not have children due to the aids virus they found in my lover's body. We were also told that if we were going to be with each other sexually that we needed to wear protection. But, me growing up in a very spirit fill home, where we were taught the word of God and to believe it; so knowing that the word of God said that all things were possible to them that believed. [Mark 9:23] Also, I was reminded of the scripture that said, the unbelieving husband is sanctified by the wife, and the unbelieving wife is sanctified by the husband: else were your children unclean, but now are they holy [I Corinthians 7:14]. The way I saw this scripture was, if he couldn't believe then I could, and I did. When the doctor told us the news and I got over the shock of it all, I began to fast and pray, crying out to God the way my mother had taught me. I'll never forget the day I drove over to my mothers house for twelve noon prayer, and while in prayer she said, "Shun, the Lord said you can't depend on mothers prayers anymore, but now you've got to know him for yourself," and I had not told her anything, I just cried even the more, asking him to heal my lover and make us whole. But it seemed like the more I prayed, things would get better and then back to worse again, but I tried to hold on.

Yet living with my grandparents we got into an argument or should I say another argument, I can't even remember what it was about, but we were yelling to the top of our voices at each other standing half chest to chest. Pressing against the other going around in circles with my pregnant self, in my spirit I had had enough of him trying to push me around, I was like come on with it, so I pushed him with my chest and said what, do something and he did.

He pushed me so hard; I fell back on the bed and flipped over to the floor. I got back up crying, later on that day the neighbor said, "I heard ya'll this morning, boy was ya'll mad." I was so hurt because we were suppose to be Christians, saved people, not caring on like sinners, but we were and we did. Little by little things can happen to you and in your life to bring you down and that's just where I was headed but I could not see it.

I would see myself and I hated what I saw, my marriage was turning me into something I never was. I was beginning to loose respect for him, which made me not want to obey him or listen to anything he had to say. He was my manager and he managed my sisters also, I would disrespect him in front of them and others which made them do the same thing. Husbands and wives if you ever loose RESPECT for each other and God don't help you, it's over. Well one night my granddaddy put us out of his house, something had went on between him and my love concerning money and helping with the bills, which I thought we were doing. Anyway we were out, me, him and the baby I was carrying along with the groceries we had bought. Because my lover said, "If I go, then my food goes with me," so we went in the lateness of the night, in my bed clothes. My cousin had an apartment that she had gotten through a government program, the way we found out about it was when we called my mother to let her know what had happened, she then told us about my cousin's place. So when we talked to my cousin about our situation, she said, "I'm hardly there any way," and she gave us the key to move in that night. The neighborhood was a very bad place, one of the worse in the city, known for drugs, robbery, you name it, it was there, if it wasn't, then it was coming (smile) (joke). I was very afraid to be there with the both of us there and especially when he went to work, I would be there all by myself.

While we were living there we had a death in the family, grandmother passed away, the one I use to keep, my daddy's mother, the wife of my granddaddy who put us out. She wasn't living there at the house, because my daddy went and got his mother took her to his house to take care of her, needless to say it was very hard on me. I don't know what happened, but to this day it is still unclear to me, but again something went down with money again, we only had to pay fifty dollars a month and my cousin said we had missed a payment and things were blown out of proportion.

We went to my aunt's house to try and work things out, but to no avail. She was cooking breakfast when we got there, we walked in, went to the back to the kitchen, sat down at the table and began to talk, I don't know how the number jumped from fifty dollars to ninety some dollars, but it did. My love started raising his voice, my aunt started raising her voice and I was sitting there praying and watching my aunt and the hot boiler of grits she was stirring. Let me tell you about my aunt whose last name was Gamble, now everybody from Poole-Creek to Plunkette Town knew that you did not mess with Inez Gamble-Couch or anything connected to her, or it was big trouble. They were known for throwing things and shooting if necessary or whatever it took for you to know that they meant business. That was what they did. Any way my aunt got to walking back and forward in front of the stove, she would put her hands on the boiler handle and then take it off, she did this about three times. The spirit spoke to me and said she want to throw those grits on your lover. I began to pray harder and binding the devil, she then turned the burner off and moved the pot altogether, I took a small sigh and said under my breath to myself, "Thank You JESUS! Then, that's when I broke my silence and said, "honey, just pay the money and let's go, we are God's children and He's gonna handle it," my aunt said, "we're God's children," and I said no, "we are all God's creation, but we all are not his children." So we left and went back to pack, we were again asked to leave another place of living, where to now, you're right, my mother's.

Well, we got settled in, by now I was at least seven months into my pregnancy, we moved into the living room/dining room, at this time we had moved from Poole Creek (Hapeville, Ga.) to College Park, Ga., in a nice up stairs and down stairs house, where you could get to the basement from the inside of the house or the outside. I thought we were somebody. Now I'm right back at the house where my lover use to date me, isn't life strange. My lover could not stand my mother and look where we ended up. We couldn't go to his mother because she was way down deep south and his job and life was in Georgia, beside we didn't have enough money to move into another apartment or anywhere, so my parents let us live there rent free, saying we could give something if we had it. Things were going good so I thought, for me anyway, shoot, I was with my folks and he seemed to be adjusting pretty much.

Now that I've matured in life and learned a few things, he could not have been happy knowing that he had to move into the house of the parents of his wife, when he was suppose to be the bread winner of the family and now he's living under another man's roof, not just any man, but his wife's Daddy. He kept a good attitude about the situation to me, he would cook dinner for the family and he could cook very well. We would eat together, watch television together, and pray together in the area where there was a fire place and a breakfast bar. It was the den, oh see in Poole Creek we didn't have a den, but the College Park house was big and nice, down stairs my daddy built three more rooms. We had a ball, people would come over for cook outs, family gatherings and on Sundays we always had a crowd over, we were the preacher's children, so we always kept people around us; mean while back to the story. Any man in the position of living with someone else with his family feels like he's not a man or that he's not taking care of what's his. I wish that I could have been a better wife all the way around. There were times when he wanted me to go on an engagement and I'd say, "I need to ask my brother first, and see if my sisters didn't have to go out of town, and if they didn't then I would do what he asked. Then, there were times I disrespected him in front of my family, no matter what he wasn't doing at home, I should have done the right thing, but being newly married and wanting attention as well as manipulating him, trying to control him to do things I wanted. So, I would snap at him, ignore him if he called me to say something to me. I told him that if things aren't right at home, then please do not get me in public and act like things are hunky dory, because I will not put on an act, so if you don't want me to act up, don't come kissing and hugging on me. Sometimes I would over spend the budget, when he specifically said to me that we didn't have it to spend, but I felt like, I made it, and can spend it. But that is not the way a save wife is suppose to behave. And talking about attitude, child I could get one, and keep it till I just couldn't keep it any more, and mood swings, there wasn't enough rope to swing my moods on; then on top of dealing with me, he was manager of my sisters, so he had to deal with nine different spirits, attitudes and moods and some of them were worse than mine. When he was with them there was no cooperation and when he got home to me there was none, what's a man to do? I wasn't a nasty person, just nice nasty.

Women, if you are not obeying your husband and you say you are saved: You're not. Wives submit yourselves unto your own husbands, as unto the Lord for the husband is the head of the wife, even as Christ is the head of the church: and he is the savior of the body [Ephesians 5:22-23]. If you're stubborn, and rebellious, the word of God says you may as well be dealing in witchcraft, iniquity and idolatry [I Samuel 15:23]. I'm not trying to hurt anybody or make you angry. I'm just telling the truth on me and if the truth hits you, then get it right, please don't let the sun go down on you in sin, and you wake up in shame. He/She that hath an ear let them hear what the Spirit is saying. It may be that there's a chance you can save your marriage.

It's 'TIME"

It's time, laying on the bed I felt this strange feeling, so I went to the bathroom, and when I finished my business (smile) I noticed a big clog of this mucus like stuff on the tissue, by this time I was standing up, I was through using the restroom so I thought, until water begin to run down my legs on it's on. I went into the room where my mother was laying down taking a nap. My love and my sisters were in the studio finishing up their album, so I woke my mother with the question, "mother what happens when your water breaks?" she then began to tell me all that happens and as she was telling me my eyes were getting bigger, by this time she jumped straight up in the bed and I was nodding my head up and down in a yes motion, she said, "It's happened," I said, "yes, ma'am," she said, "calm down, call your doctor, take a bath, I'll call the studio and get your suitcase." So off to the hospital we went, they prepared me and got me ready for delivery, the hours were long but the actual delivery was short, I thought it was going to be worse than what it was, I was scared, I heard other women screaming saying, "doctor, please come take this thing out of me," they were saying lots of stuff. It was like going to the dentist and all the other children are yelling and screaming so you're thinking, I'm gonna be screaming and yelling too, it's going to hurt, but until you get to the back your-self, only then will you know the truth of the whole matter. I remember seeing on television the wives yelling at their husbands, saying all kind of mean things to them, but I didn't experience that, I guess I had done It so much before until I didn't need to do it here (smile), there is so much to tell, I just can't tell it all.

Well here she is four pounds and ten ounces, the doctor did not have to spank her because upon arrival she cried just a little, I was watching here as the doctor held her up and after she did her little cry, she looked around the entire room as if she knew where she was and her eyes looked like as if she was saying, "Okay, I'm here and I know what I'm suppose to do." I said to myself, this girl acts like she knows where she is, we named her, Xenia Pace Rhodes.

We'll talk about her death later on, but for now I must tell you about her life. Oh, how happy I was to know that I had given birth to a little girl, happy is really not the word, I can't tell you how I felt, the love, oh the love, no mother in this entire world love's their children more than I love mine (ooh, look at you, I knew that I would get that response, good, that means you're just like me, smile). You love your child/children just like I do.

Xenia couldn't go home right away do to yellow jaundice. I didn't want to leave but the doctor made me go home. Everyday I was up there in time for the feedings, I would sit in the nursery and sing to her as I fed her, I did this for two days, on the second day the doctor said, "good news Tarrian, you can take your baby home", this was on a Sunday and everybody was at church and the doctor had advised me not to be at home alone, so to church we went. Straight from the hospital, she was only two days old. That Sunday we had a guest minister and his church visiting from Baltimore, MD. And when they say Xenia they immediately fell in love with her, so right then and there I asked them if they would be her god parents and they said, "Yes". Bishop and Lady E. We left church early and went home. My lover was so proud to be a daddy and he loved, loved, loved his little girl and worked hard for us, the best he could and for that I love him, Thank You.

Things were like a ride at an amusement park, one time you're up and next you're leveled, then all of a sudden the drop hits you and all you can do is just stay on the ride until it's over.

One day, my mother came to me, who is a prophetess herself

and a true one, this I know. She came in where we were living and said to me, "Shun, there's something I need to tell you; I'm telling you this first, because the Lord said you can take it and secondly you need to know", a funny feeling hit the pit of my stomach, then I said, "mother, yes ma'am, I'm listening", her next words were, "your love is cheating on you, I don't know how long it's been going on, but I do know that it happened, besides the Lord telling me, he gave me proof". She said that one day my love offered her a ride in our car to take here to the store and as he opened the door for her, she noticed a condom on the floor of the car and it was freshly used. She asked him, "son, what is that?"

While looking at it, replying he didn't know, but at the same time reaching to pick it up, she said, "no son, if you don't know what it is don't touch it, germs could be all over it," he then went to get some paper to pick it up and throw it away. The proof that the Lord revealed to my mother was during our church choir workshop, which was conducted by two well known persons in the gospel music industry. I was out of town and he didn't want to miss the workshop so he stayed home, besides he was one of the directors at the church. My mother told him what the Lord had said and what went on one night after the workshop and he said, "Oh, no! That didn't happen," then she said, "Oh yes! It did son and it happened Wednesday night. Now, which one of the guest you were with I don't know, but it did happen." She said he fell to his knees and said, "You are right mother," he repented and said he was sorry; yet she told him again to tell me or she was going to tell me. She said to him, "Son, if my daughter catch aids and die as much as I love the Lord you're going to have trouble out of me. (she said, a law-suit) Now I'm going to give you time to tell Shun and if you haven't told her, then I'm going to tell her".

I remember one day sitting at home mad at my lover about something that he didn't do, (I don't quite remember what it was) but the phone rung and I answered it with a very harsh tone, "Hello!" the voice on the other end inquired, "Mother Pace," and I said, "She ain't here," then he said, "Shun," and I said, "yes, this is she," I then recognized that it was the voice of the Prophet who had ministered to us once before, who is now my god daddy, then he said, "you're the one I'm trying to reach, what's wrong? The Lord put you in my spirit." I then began to cry, telling him everything, from the very first phone call about the doctor finding the aids virus in his body, to cheating on me and everything, I said, "I hate him, and I wish he was dead," he said to me, "that ain't God, and its witchcraft." He proceeded to talk to me and pray for me and my love. The prophet instructed me to tell my lover some things that the Lord had spoken to him. He said, "I don't care if he falls in the floor kicking and screaming like a spoiled brat, you tell him what I said." He also told me that somebody had been praying for my lover and what the doctors thought they saw, God had not allowed it to activate in his body, but if he slip one time, that what the doctors had seen, God was going to allow it to activate and take him out of here.

Well, wouldn't you know it, when my love got home, I told him what the man of God told me to tell him and he fell in the floor kicking and screaming and beating the floor liked a spoiled brat. I sat on the bed looking down at him laughing, I could not believe my eyes. To myself I said the man of God was right. When he got up I told him that the Prophet said that you were going to do everything you just did and he said, "I am sick of the prophet and your mother."

I was told by my nephew that my lover approached him one Sunday morning before we all left to go to church, my nephew was down stairs and my lover had to go get something out of the dryer, that's when it happen and he begged my nephew not to tell me, but he did tell my mother. I remember coming from church one night and my lover said he had to go to the restroom real bad and he couldn't hold it, so he suggested upon arriving at the exit of a certain Hotel he said that this would be a good place to stop because he had to go just that bad, So parking at the hotel he got out and went in, he stayed so long I fell asleep, woke up and he still wasn't in the car, drifting back off to sleep I was awakened by him getting in the car explaining to me why it took him so long. All these incidents took place while living with my parents and I didn't find out about some of these things until I was divorced.

We stayed with my parents until Xenia was two years old and then we moved. We heard that a mother in the church was renting her house, 2481 Old Tony Rd. Ellenwood, GA. Three bedrooms, living room, dining room, kitchen and bathroom, a real nice cozy house, just right for the three of us. I went in pulling up carpet, painting, striping cabinets, retiling the kitchen floor, putting up mirrors, paneling and you name it I was doing it, we had a nice place when we finished or should I say I finished my lover said to me go head honey, your mama and daddy taught you well, I just smiled, Xenia had her own room pink and white with all white furniture which her God parents bought, she was a blessed little girl, my concert dates had picked up a little, making more money, thank you Jesus! If she wanted it, and God provided it, she got it.

Things were going well, even though we were renting, it was a place where we could be on our own and be a family with just the three of us together. Every newlywed couples, and newly families need space to breath and grow and get to know one another (let the church say, Amen) in a place of their own. Xenia was two years old, when I and my love was out of town on an engagement, on our way back home we stopped in Charlotte, N.C. to use the phone to check our voice mail; he always checked it, faithfully. Anyway one of the messages was my mother telling us that Xenia had received the Holy Ghost. He beckoned for me to come to the phone to hear what my mother had said. We then called home to speak directly to her and while talking to her, she said if she wasn't there to witness it herself, she wouldn't believe it if someone had told her too; but she said Shun, your baby has been filled with the Holy Ghost at the age of two, I was crying and praising God. After calming down I asked how it happened, what was she doing? She said, "they were listening to Rev. J. C. singing, 'There is lifting for me'", during this time Rev. C. was in the hospital, but the wonderful and strange thing that happened to me was, while carrying Xenia at seven months, singing at the E. H. music and arts seminar, after I had sang Rev. C. saw me sitting on a park bench, he stopped his car, got out and touched my stomach and complimented me on my singing while I was pregnant, I felt special because it was Rev. C. touching me and my baby. While visiting out in California again, we went to Rev. C's church one Sunday morning, he asked me to sing during the service and I did the song "Safe in his Arms", after I finished Rev. C. picked the song back up and began to minister prophetically saying, the Lord said somebody needs a healing in their body and if you would just get up and walk the floor—healing would come. I began to walk the floor when I noticed my love sitting; I went over to him and said we need to be walking. And we did as the man of god instructed. Then Rev.C said for us to bring Xenia to him, she was six months. He held her up over his white marble communion table which had a red velvet cloth down the middle, with two candles and one gold cross. He christened Xenia that Sunday morning saying "Lord, we give thee Xenia, in the name of Jesus Amen".

I can recall when Rev. C. passed, because Xenia was sitting in the floor listening to the radio, when one of his songs began to play and she began to weep bitterly, with her head back and then she dropped forward to her chest, I knew that something had happened, then the radio personality said,

"We are sorry to announce that Rev. C. passed away and we are going to miss him. Xenia was a very special girl, and what was the connection between her and Rev. C. only God knew. Xenia had four sets of god parents.

Things were going fine, then the arguments started back up, only this time it was more than money, it was about him coming home late leaving me all day with nothing but hot pockets, I hot pocketed all day, then when he would come home, he would bring me a sandwich from a burger joint, this happened also when I was pregnant, no wonder Xenia only weighed four pounds and ten ounces (smile). Some nights when he would come home late I would try to turn him on so that we could be together as husband and wife, but the more I'd try, the more he would reject me, this happened many times. Some times he would go for months without touching me, I thought something was wrong with me, and when he wanted me it was only to his satisfaction, I couldn't even call him the minute man; as I later found out what this phrase meant. All I know is I wasn't satisfied. I even struck up the conversation one day asking him was I pleasing him. He said O yes honey, then I said, well I'm not, something is missing on my end, because when it's over, I'm yet waiting for something to happen. I even asked if I needed to do something else, he said No! Honey, you don't need to do that. Once again conversation was limited and nothing was accomplished.

To me this was serious so I sought after counseling from a visiting minister and his wife, who was in revival at my parents church (who later on became my god parents) so after service that night we all talked for a long time, about every thing, when I told the preacher the length of time he wouldn't touch me, he started counting from one to ten, the preacher asked him what was he doing? My love said that he would be working late at a friends house for some music on her up coming CD, and when I get home I'm just too tired, I butted in saying but you leave at ten in the morning and don't return until two a.m. the next morning, the preacher started counting again but this time he went pass ten. He looked at my love and said, "if you aint giving it to her, then you are giving it to someone else, the room got quiet, the preacher walked out, and so did we at my loves request, we didn't go back to the revival that week. Two months later my sister called saying she needed to talk to me, she waited a day, came over, we went to a chicken place, got our food and was sitting in the car, looking at her I knew something was wrong, so I said, "what's up" (again the news I was about to hear little did I know was going to change my life, No, change my world for ever.) she said as she broke into tears our spouses has been together; I'm sitting there like, been where, for a ride in the car, out to dinner together, been where? Then she told me. She brought back to my remembrance the incident, and asked if I remembered, I said yes, she said it was then when it happened. But me being of a prideful spirit, didn't want to face that anything was wrong with my marriage, so after admitting that I knew, I said, my love told me about that and he said nothing happened, I don't want to hear any more about it, now; I don't know what you are going to do, but I'm staying with my love and I'm going to believe him, now please take me home. While riding home, I was saying to myself, I can't believe her, just because her marriage is on the rocks, I can't believe she's trying to burst up my home. But it was during these rough times of our marriage that I asked my love if we could fast and pray, seeking God to help us, well into the second day of our fast, I was going to bed, when I noticed my love eating ice cream, when I said, love we are suppose to be fasting, his reply was this is just frozen milk and kept eating. The word of the Lord reads: Can two walk together except they agree, (Amos 3:3.)

The preacher's back for revival, and this time he's at my church, we have no other choice but to go. We went every night, now here it is Sunday night the last night of the revival. About an hour before service were to begin, I got this funny feeling in the pit of my stomach like I had done something wrong and I was in trouble. After the preacher had finished ministering, he asked for my love, and where he was, I said he's in the back of the church sitting down, the man of God said come here son, come quickly! He began to minister to my love, telling him what he saw and how that different things were going to happen to him (that was not good) if he did not CHANGE!

Well, after church I was so ashamed, hurt and felt like disappearing, well that old saying is true "warning before destruction, we all get them, but do we pay attention to them? Riding in the car on the way home neither of us talked to each other for awhile, I then said honey, what was God saying to you? And what have you done to make God say what he said through the preacher? Is there something you need to tell me? He started to talk, when I cut him off {with my left hand raised} and said don't say anything to me because I don't want you to start lying to me, just write it down in a letter and I will read it later. This was Thursday night, he was getting ready to go to Muscle Shoals, AL. to mix my second album entitled "Shekinah Glory".

The next day before he gave me the letter and asked me honey, after you read it, are you gonna leave me; I stated, I don't know it depends on what's in it. He left to go out of town, I didn't read the letter right away I waited until 3:00 a.m. Friday morning to read the letter, which was my prayer time, so I got on my knees and said "Lord I don't know what is in this letter, but I need you to help me. I began to read the letter and once again the news I was about to read was going to change my life no, change my world, no rock my world no, was totally going to shatter me and my family and those connected to me. He said in this letter, Dear Shun, honey I know I told you that nothing happened between me and my kin, but we did have oral sex and the letter that you found in the top draw from a friend from down south, there was a relationship between the two of us as well. Going back to the incident [I can remember us being

home one night, he was in the shower and I was in Xenia's room
doing general cleaning and in a draw I stumbled across a letter from
a guy address to him; I was curious as most wives are and it made
me read this letter and in the letter he was saying he missed him and
when was he coming down to see him… I folded the letter back up
and put it in the draw and the phone rung, when I answered it and
the person heard my voice they hung up and I hung up and said who
was that, my instinct went to the letter I said, that's the guy who
wrote the letter about fifteen minutes later the phone rings again
and I answered with a stern Hello, and I got no answer and I said
hello again and then the voice called my loves name, I then said no,
this is the Mrs. then he rudely said I want to speak to (he called his
name), your husband so I walked into the bathroom with the phone
in my hand with all the attitude I could get on my face, handing him
the phone, I said who is this on the phone that's asking for you and
he's rude he asked me who was it? I stated it's the guy that wrote
the letter that I found in the top draw, his eyes bucked then he
quickly gathered his emotions and said for me to tell him that he
was in the shower and he would call him back. I relayed the
message and the rude guy just hung up without saying bye. Of
course I was filled with emotions, hot, upset, mad, angry, hurt,
bewildered (come on help me out, give me some more emotions
(smile). What I didn't want to believe was hitting me hard in the
face to the point where I could no longer deny the fact that my
husband is cheating on me]. Back to the letter, there was about ten
to twelve men names that he had listed telling me that he had been
with these guys, mind you the names that I read I couldn't believe,
because I knew everyone of these guys except for about two. A few
of them my mind went to their wives, I wondered if they knew, and
until this day I have not told any of them. [But, I do want to stop
here and take a moment and share a word with you if I may. To you
husbands and wives that are cheating on your spouses, sleeping
around with other people and then coming back home to your
spouse giving them diseases and possibly AIDS, God's ! Going to
get you!!! This comes as a warning from him. For the word of the
Lord says in Proverbs 15:3 The eyes of the Lord are in every place,
beholding the evil and the deceived and deluded and misled; God

will not allow Himself to be sneered at (scorned, disdained, or mocked by mere pretensions of professions, or by His precepts being set aside). [He inevitably deludes himself who attempts to delude God.] For whatever a man sows to his own flesh (lower nature, sensuality will from the flesh reap decay and ruin and destruction, but he who sows to the Spirit will from the Spirit reap eternal life. Romans 6:23a reads as thus, for the wages of sins pay is death. (Amplified Version); and as the version of the world "payback is a Mother".] Now back to the letter one of the guys at the night of my recording, was assisting me that night giving me water, wiping the sweat from my face, giving me juice, giving all this attention, now looking back I'm wondering if it was guilt of him knowing what he had done and probably wondering if I knew. After my love had gotten back from mixing the album, he went to the bathroom and noticed black stuff in the sink and yelled, Shun! Which woke me up; I said yes, he said, what's this here in the sink? And I got up to go see what he was talking about, and when I got there I said, oh, it's the letter you wrote. (I had destroyed the letter by burning it in the sink). Him not knowing exactly what I was going to do next, he asked me how I felt about everything that had happened. I said to him, I feel like we were climbing Mt. Everest, you had made it to the top and was getting ready to pull me up, when all of a sudden you hit me with a blow (of him cheating on me) and I fell all the way back down feeling every hit. This is how I described to him my feelings of the whole situation. And if all this drama wasn't enough, I was pregnant again with our second child. After the recording things got worse. The last argument we had was again about money, and paying off the balance of a rent to own big screen TV, during this argument I heard and saw anger that I had never seen before; we were yelling and screaming at each other again, I then told him that I couldn't take anymore and that I was going back home, all at once he jumped towards me with a quick reflex, gritting his teeth, with his hands in a fist and said to me well go home then. In spite of everything that had taken place I knew then that our marriage was over. I think the only reason he didn't hit me was, he thought about me being pregnant. After that I went into the bedroom and sat on the bed and as I looked down at my dress my stomach was trembling because of fear. I got up and went into the bathroom locked the door, put down the toilet seat and sat down, looking out of the window up towards the sky, "I said to God Lord please forgive me, but I can't take this no more, please just let them find me in time to save my baby, I then looked for the knife that we always kept in the bathroom from Xenia, because it was a very sharp knife and we didn't want her to get hurt. But to my surprise I couldn't find the knife anywhere, "did it just disappear?" or did he move it? Where is that knife? Were the thoughts going through my head, by this time I sat back down and said to myself, lord where is the knife? Then, I heard a loud bang on the door, bang, bang, bang, bang, Shun open this door screamed my love, which scared me then I said no, go away, I ain't coming out, he banged even harder, then it got quiet for a moment then I heard another type of noise at the door, it was him trying to pick the lock open, he got in and as soon as he stepped in, I went out, noticing that he had the knife in his hand, crying fake tears he tried to talk to me but I wasn't hearing him at this point, walking fast as I could out of the bathroom, up the hall, through the kitchen and out the side door to the back of the house, leaning against the house crying and scared at the same time because I thought that he was going to follow me but he didn't, so I broke down then because I was free to let my tears flow, I looked up towards heaven crying, I said Lord, you've got to help me, I can't take this no more, all at once the sun got brighter and from the sun I heard a voice say to me You will **NEVER** go through this again. Such a peace came over me, I began to smile while looking at the sun, only then was I able to go back into the house because I knew down on the inside that everything was going to be alright, now I didn't know how long it was going to take before everything was alright but all I knew was HE told me, and that was it. Within a few moments I heard a car pull up into the driveway, it was my cousin, I heard him talking to my sister Leslie who was spending the night with me, I'm so sorry that she had to witness all of this I can see her face now, she was sitting in a chair in the living room when we started fussing and she had the face of a little girl who's parents were fighting, so she got out of the way and just sat there quietly, anyway she asked him what made you come over? He said, I was thinking about "LayShun (is how they say it, it's really LaShun) and here I am, now I knew it was God working but I had to be wise, I didn't move a muscle because I knew if he had came in and saw me the way I was, he and my love would have been at it, and I didn't want that so I just listened to him and my sister talk, my sister ended the conversation by saying, well Charles so good to see you, but we alright, he said are you sure, by this time I was saying, in the room, yes Charles please now go! Leslie, said yea we alright and he left. My love stayed around for a while what he was doing I can't even remember, I do know that latter on he took a shower and left, my sister upon my request started gathering some of my things, its was around three o'clock that evening or later, anyway while I was packing another sister came over Phyllis, for no reason just like my cousin did, only this time I left with her, but the strange thing was my sister Leslie stayed behind why, I didn't know then, but now I do, I think God had her to do this so that when he got back from where ever he had gone he wouldn't blow up even more, by him seeing her there he thought I would return, NOT! Baby, I was gone not to return, I kept holding on to the voice that told me you'll never go through this again. So here I am back at my parents again but this time on my own with my first born Xenia, 3 years old and the baby I was caring; Lord, what am I to do now? He did everything for me, paid bills, ironed my clothes, washed dishes if I didn't feel like it, ran my bath water, did all the driving, prepared everything for all my live recording sessions, all I had to do was to consecrate myself and show up and sang. But, now everything rested upon my shoulders, thrust into a world I had no clue about, eight years of having someone there doing the buck of everything and then to have it taken away, sort of feels like two people on a see / saw and the person at the other end quickly, and suddenly jumps off while your end is up in the air it's all done so fast until the next thing you know your mouth is open and your butt is on the ground and boy does it hurt, but there is nothing you can do because, first of all you were not expecting for it to happen, and then you couldn't believe that the other person could have been thinking to do such a thing, but you get up and go on. I thought it would be a quick divorce but he contested it I guess he was thinking that only because of the position I was in, one lap baby and one on the way, but I said what good would it do for them to see and hear us fussing and fighting, besides the love, and the respect had gone.

Sitting in church one night thinking about my situation, I thought about one of my god daddies Bishop K. B., so later that week I called him, we talked for a while, he then told me about a book entitled "The Compassionate side of Divorce", he also said to me, now some churches are not going to let you sing or preach in them because of how they feel about the subject but you have got to know what God said and hold on to that and all other man made religion he said for me to "Run over". In this book they asked a question, when does a person become a robber? And they had a picture of a man lying in bed thinking about the robbery and another picture of a man in the very act of robbing, I picked the second one because he was actually doing the robbing, but the answer was the first man the one who was thinking of robbing, and they gave the scripture about, as a man thinketh in his heart then so is he. [Proverbs 23:7 for as he thinketh in his heart, so is he:] then they asked another question, when does a couple becomes divorced? When the judge grants it and give the papers or the moment he/she had the thoughts of being unfaithful to their spouse? Yes, it's the very moment that the thought was conceived in your mind and you didn't cast it out in the powerful name of Jesus, but you entertained the thought and let it nest there until it hatched. As the preachers say, don't raise your hands; but how many of you who are married, are unfaithful to your spouse, because you've thought about sleeping with "Sally or Bob", anyway, this book was a big part of my healing. I remember asking my love when did he start messing around. He said it was two years after we were married, well now where was I? I even asked him before you took your clothes off did I come cross your mind one time?

You know what, now I know why he didn't like me looking at O everyday, and I mean everyday, because when he got home from wherever, I would tell him, you know today O said this that and the other, and especially the times she would talk about cheating spouses, when I brought that up that's when he said to me that O is going to get you in trouble. I say if being a better person, a stronger person, and having self confident is trouble then I like that kind of trouble; with God and O (smile) I'm a better woman. Well, I can't leave out my praying mother, daddy, family, church, and friends, and my god parents, and prayer warriors who prayed for me when I didn't know they were praying for me. Thank you Mom T and Mama S, I love you.

The Separation/Divorce

I'm back at home, trying to regroup and deal with the separation of my love, which eventually ended up in divorce. But God used Phyllis and her love for the game Scrabble to keep our minds from dwelling on what we were going through, for the few years we were at home; we would play scrabble all day long, everyday; Yes, God was our keeper and our healer, and we were surround by prayer, but I feel as I said early, that God used Phyllis and scrabble as well to help with our healing process.

I had to continue traveling even though I was pregnant, going from state to state, and city to city. But God would speak to me some profound things at different times during my travel. And I knew it was God because it was no way possible I could think of these things on my on; I can remember in New Jersey, laying in the bed and one morning the Lord woke me up out of my sleep, and said to me; le me show you how God I am; I said I'm listening Lord; he went on to say, I will take a man's family from him, and make him watch me give it to another man; that's how God I am.

Another time the Lord spoke to me, it was in question form; he asked, how does a man and woman (married) become one? I said through blood upon intercourse; he then asked me another question, he said do you remember when I said that I sanctified your blood? I said, yes Lord, he said well everything and anything that had to do with your love has been washed out of your body; then he said something that blew my mind, he said in the Spirit you are a virgin all over again, because the blood I put in you has not been mixed with any man's blood on earth. Now to me that was powerful because I had been feeling like I was so unclean, and that no man would ever want me, or even look my way, I just felt dirty, but God knows where you are in times and periods of your life, and will meet you right there and give you everything you need. After that I felt like I was worth something, not to man; but to God; it was then, for the first time I felt like I belonged, if no one loved me, God does.

The Arrival of Aarion

July 20, 1993, It's a girl! Yes, God gave me another girl, which was what I wanted. It was like twenty eight hours of labor; someone, I don't know who or how they found out that the gospel singer LaShun Pace was having a baby, and her family was in the room with her, so they wanted them to sing. Can you imagine me in labor, doing my breathing and my family singing, "Amazing Grace" I was like hello, I'm trying to have a baby here can the concert wait? But, it was truly amazing when Aarion Mychkiel Pace graced the world with her presence. Yea, I gave her my maiden name, only because I was bitter, angry and mad at my love, so I was trying to prove a point, it was a power game or a power move, I' m just keeping it real. But since then she has taken on her rightful name Aarion Mychkiel Rhodes. But let's go back to the time before Aarion was born. I was around seven and a half months pregnant when my love asked me to let Xenia go with him to his home town since she wasn't going to be in our friends wedding, and that they would be back within two weeks or so. So, I didn't see the harm in letting her go, I was about to give birth within a few weeks, and I would need the time with a new baby on my hands, so I packed Xenia's things and off they went down south to his mothers house. Of course I would call Xenia to see how she was doing, to let her know that her mommy loved her very much and that she would see me and her baby sister or brother real soon, she had told me that she wanted a little sister, so that's what I started saying to her, you'll see me and your little sister soon. There were times when I called that they would tell me that Xenia would be playing with her dolls calling them her sister. Well weeks went by and then months, I was told that Xenia had began to ask questions about when was she coming home to me and her sister, I don't know what they told her but they did tell me that she had started asking a lot of questions concerning coming home. One time I called down there to speak to her and they would not let her come to the phone, (I was talking to his mother), so I asked her why wouldn't she put Xenia on the phone? And she started breathing funny and stuff, so I asked her if her son had told her not to let me speak to Xenia? And she said yes, and I asked why? She said that he said that every time I'd call and speak to her that when we would hang up, that Xenia would cry and say that she misses me, and he did not want her going through those changes like that, and that from now on just don't let her talk to me whenever I would call. Can you imagine that, not being able to talk to your own baby, when you can hear her voice in the background, oh how my heart ached, I started crying on the phone, but she still wouldn't let me speak to my child. One time I called and I tried to appeal to the mother side of her (his mom) but to no avail, I even asked her to put herself in my shoes, still nothing. This went on for weeks, now by this time I was ready to fight, pregnant and all, I was ready to walk down there and get my child. So I asked my daddy could I use his car that the church had just bought him and he said No, because he didn't want any trouble. Looking back, now I know that it wasn't God's time yet. But one night while on my knees praying, at this time I had given birth to Aarion, she was about two weeks old. It was almost midnight when the Lord said to me, Go and get your child now! I jumped up immediately from my knees, went up into the living room where my daddy was sleeping, he and my mother moved out of their room just for me so that me and my baby could have a nice place to sleep. Anyway, I asked if I could use his car again to go and get Xenia, and without hesitating he said yea, go head. Phyllis and Latrice, along with me and Aarion got in the car and took off. It was a twelve hour trip; we got there around eleven thirty that morning. Now the motivation for me going to get my child was, they wasn't letting me talk to my baby, secondly he wanted a ransom in exchanged for my daughter, he told me that the only reason he hadn't brought her home was that he needed gas money; and I said that he could borrow some money from your mother or your aunt. He then said to me no, if you just pay me my half from the engagement he had booked before we were separated, and then maybe I'll bring her back. I felt like, I'm on my own now, and I needed all the money I could get and I thought he didn't deserve anything, besides he had gotten a job, and had put Xenia in school, third, she was getting ready to turn five, last but not least, God had told me to go and get her. So from these things I knew he had no intentions of bringing her back home. They would say to me when I would call, how much my baby had grown, and that she's this, and she's that, which made my heart sadder. I would sit in my rocking chair, starring at the mirror where I had put Xenia's picture, praying and crying, asking God to please move so that I may see my daughter again. Well here we are, the Lord gave us safe travel, and not knowing when my love was going to work, I told my sister to take me to a pay phone and let me call to the house to see what was going on. So, I called and his mother answered, we talked for a while, then I asked to speak to Xenia knowing that he had told them not to let her come to the phone, and the next voice I heard was his, saying didn't I tell you Shun, that I did not want her to talk to you, because she goes through too many changes after she talks to you, then I said, if you bring her home she wouldn't have to go through nothing.

He knew that my sisters were working on their album, so he asked sarcastically how were things going with them, see he use to manage me and my sisters but now all of that was taken away, I said that things were going well, and that they had a rehearsal that evening, he had no clue that I was right there in the city coming for my child; then he said to me that he had to go and get ready for work, we hung up, I got back in the car, told them what was said and everything. We then drove to a church parking lot up the street from where they lived so we could see their house, I felt like we were on a stake out or something. Our plan was to call for a taxi to take me to the house, while they filled the car up with gas; I would get Xenia, jump in the taxi and come back to where they were parked, then we'd take off back to Atlanta a different way than we had come. But things didn't work out the way we had planed. We called the taxi, and when he came I, (Ms. Got to tell it all) started telling him our plans, he looked confused, and then told us that he wanted nothing to do with what was going on, I guess I gave him (**t.m.i.**) too much information. So there we were no taxi, low on gas, and I had to use it, and scared, so I told my sister to take me some where to use the restroom, but I was in such a tight I couldn't hold it, so I went right there in the middle of the street on one of the back roads from their house, I finished just in time when a car with all guys came riding by; boy my sisters were laughing at me, but I didn't care, cause I was free to do what I had come to do, bring my child back home. So we went back to our little stake out and kept watching the house, Phyllis said to me, what if he back out the drive way and head this way? I looked with my eyes bucked and said we'll just all have to duck until he pass by, then Latrice said, he doesn't know this car, he only knows what the old car looks like. There he is coming out of the house going to his car, he pulls out and goes the other way, and we waited about a good fifteen minutes or so just to make sure he didn't leave anything and had to come back. Well here it goes, we were creeping up to the house, we stopped one house away from their house and I walked the rest of the way. I made it to the front door and began to knock, his mother answered, I said hello, she seemed surprised and began to unlock the door saying hey, I thought you were in Atlanta and here you are, all while she was talking I was watching her hands as she was unlocking the door to let us in, I was saying to myself, she's really letting us in. At this point Xenia looked and saw that it was me at the door and began to scream with joy Mommy! Mommy! then she began to cry at the same time, then I started crying too, and calling her name, Xenia baby, I cried for two reasons one, I was happy and excited to see my child, two, from the way she looked, her clothes were too little for her and her hair wasn't combed, eating a peach with juice dripping all over her clothes. This was not how I kept my daughter looking, but at the same time I didn't care I just wanted my baby. I was going towards the couch to sit down trying to keep things cool when Latrice who was standing on the outside said, Shun, what are you doing? Get Xenia and let's go! By now his mother was having a fit saying NO! NO! Ya'll can't do this, I said yes I can! She's my daughter; she said well let me clean her up, I said I'll clean her up when she gets home, she said well can't you wait until her daddy gets back? I and Latrice said at the same time NO! She grabbed Xenia's arm and I had the other one, Xenia was crying and calling my name Mommy, we were outside at this time. Latrice was trying to help me get Xenia from his mother, but she wouldn't turn Xenia a loose, I was pulling Xenia from behind, his mother was in front pulling, and Latrice had his mom around the waist pulling her from Xenia, when Tricee's foot went into a hole in their yard amongst the fake planted grass, that's when she and his mother fell. Me being just two weeks post pardon I had very little strength, when they fell she lost the grip on Xenia's arms, but she caught a hold of her legs, it was a hot July day, and not having enough strength the sun was beating down on me, and I said to Tricee, I can't do it I'm too weak, she said pull Shun! By this time I cried out Lord, you've got to help me and Xenia's legs just slipped through her hands as if oil was on her legs. I picked Xenia up from the ground and we ran down the street to the car and Latrice followed. Every body is safely in the car, Phyllis was holding Aarion crying, I quickly grabbed her, so that we could go and away we went going back another route. Xenia asked, is that my sister? I said with tears in my eyes, yes baby, this is your sister. She then wanted to hold her, while holding her she said my sister, my baby, we all just cried; we were so happy to have Nia back with us. Suddenly we heard a bell bing, bing, bing, bing, silence filled the car as we all saw the message center reading "miles to empty, 0" (zero). We were at least forty five to fifty miles away from the nearest gas station, we pulled off the highway to use one of those emergency phones but it wasn't working, we asked a truck driver who had pulled over, for help and he couldn't, we got back on the highway and I started questioning Phyllis about why didn't she do this, that and the other concerning the gas, when the Lord said to me, "if you want me to help you then shut up and start praying", I shut my mouth and did as He told me, then he said to me you all are going to make it but I don't want you to ever bring it up or say who's fault it was, I said yes Lord. We made it! Thank You Jesus!!! And to this day whenever we talk about it, and they get on the gas part, I just hush and keep my cool. Later, I found out from a friend (Soul) who said to me, I always knew that you were a woman of God, but now I know for sure, he then went on to tell me that my love had called him and said that he was getting ready to sue me for abandonment, because I had not seen Xenia in three months nor had I sent any money to him to take care of her. I could not believe what I heard, but I'm sure he was cooking up something or else the Lord would not have told me to go and get her. He is an on time God; always in time, just right for my time, Jesus. Needless to say my love was hot when his mother told him that I had just left their house and that Xenia was with me. I really felt good about everything; I had my girls with me. Xenia held Aarion in her lap all the way home. After, we had gotten home Xenia began to ask questions about me and her daddy, with her getting ready to celebrate a birthday, I quickly jumped the subject by asking her what would she want for her birthday? It worked.

It's August thirty first, "Happy Birthday Xenia!" boy did we have a good time, the only strange thing was that Xenia was five, and all of her guest with the exception of about three was the age of ten to forty, she never really had children her age as friends, to her they were babies (smile). Xenia has always had an old spirit; she had the characteristic of a church mother and wisdom to go with it.

Well, I thought that the birthday conversation we had would take her mind off of our family situation but it didn't; by this time we had been to court and the judge had awarded me full custody of the girls and awarded him visitation every first and third weekends, but Aarion didn't have to go until she was two, he also had to pay two hundred dollars a month Child support, for both girls together. I asked the judge if he would at least wait until Aarion was five, but he said no, for a while Xenia was going to visitation all alone without her sister and she began to cry because she did not want to leave her baby, watching her get into the car crying, was heart breaking to me as a mother, plus in the back of my mind was the question, what if they decide to keep her again? Or run off with her? And when the day came for the both of them to go to visitation it was dramatic for all of us, Aarion screaming to the top of her lungs, yelling and kicking, calling for me, and Xenia started crying and going through changes from watching Aarion. This went on for every first and third weekend that God allowed to come, and my heart was getting heavier each time, (now I can imagine Xenia's little heart enlarging each time from all the sadness she had to deal with.) yes, she loved her daddy but she didn't want to go over all the time, she wanted to go only when she wanted to, not forced to go. I would cry, praying God to please do something to stop this, Lord you see they don't like going on visitation weekends, I need for you to move. I prayed this prayer for about five years, but there were no change. So, I tried to help the Lord out, I started keeping them away on visitation or when I had to go out of town I wouldn't tell my family so that way the girls would miss going all together. I really didn't care about the law at that time all I was trying to do is make my girls happy. Honestly, I wasn't trying to hurt him, I just could not take seeing and hearing the torture each time, having to watch that car drive away hearing the screams of my children as they drove off saying, Mommy help me, I don't wanna go, God! HELP ME!!! Was what I would say each time, and to me it seemed like He just wasn't listening. But now knowing what I know, He was listening all the time; it just wasn't time for him to move yet. The Holy Spirit gave me something special one day for me and my girls, which I call M.D.T. "Mother and daughter time". MDT consisted of us talking at the end of the day, we would get on the bed in a circle and just talk about any and everything from A to Z, you name it and we talked about it. Well, the questions started up again, this time Xenia wanted to know exactly what did her daddy do, was the question she asked, and why can't we get back together again? So I told him about the questions and concerns that she had and he said to me that he would tell her in his own time. Aarion wasn't old enough to know anything yet. So, I gave him several visitation weekends, which I thought was plenty of time for him to tell her himself and not to hear it from people in the church, because church people can be something else, not the saints, but "Church" people. I'm not happy to say this, but the church is supposed to be a place where you can get help, not get hurt.

Well, he hasn't told her yet; One night, like every night Xenia and I was watching cable television, one movie had went off and another one was coming on, it was a special about couples with the same sex, in relationships together.

So, I looked at her and said, alright it's time to get to bed, get on your side and turn towards the wall and go to sleep. She did as I requested, but when she got under the covers, and turned over, the Lord spoke to me and said, this is your chance; you asked me to give you how to tell her, now is the time; let her watch this special. She watched it from start to finish, and at the very end there were two men sitting together, and the two men started going towards each other, getting closer to each others mouths, and then it faded to black. Looking at her facial expressions, I said to her, Xenia do you remember asking mommy about what your daddy did and why we can't get back together again? She said, yes mam, I said to her well, what you just saw those two men doing is what daddy did; so that's why we can't get back together. Then she said to me, my daddy was kissing men? I said yes baby, she said; and I quote her words exactly, "that's disgusting". I think I opened up a can of worms, because she went back on the next visitation talking about what she had seen, and what I had told her concerning him, my, my, my, was he upset; he called me asking me why did I tell her those things about him. And that he was going to tell her when he got good and ready. I told him that I had given him time to tell her, and that he had plenty of chances, but he didn't do it so I did, and I felt that it was my responsibility as her mother to give her answers to all of her questions.

As time moved on their daddy would take me back and forth to court, trying to get full custody of them, trying to prove that I was an unfit mother; and the tool he was trying to use most was me traveling. I was the soul provider for my children, so therefore I had to get out there and make some money to feed us and give a little something to my parents, whom I stayed with for a while, and then we moved in with my sister Duranice for a while, and then we moved in with another sister for a while, June. No, they didn't charge me rent or anything, but I would give something when ever I had it to spare. Besides, he wasn't paying child support like he should have, but I didn't do anything, I should have, but why should you have to make a person do the right thing by their own children? But, like I said, I was on the road a lot and Phyllis "auntie mommy", my mother, June, Duranice and my family, would take turns keeping my girls, but for the most part they were with Phyllis, to whom I also gave something for keeping them. As I said earlier, the only reason I wasn't homeless was because of family.

While I was on the road he was taking me to court and I had no idea, so me not showing up for the court dates; really looked bad on my part, anyway this resulted in a bench warrant for my arrest. So I called my lawyer one night, and she told me girl if you are ever caught in a road block, or pulled over for a ticket, or anything; they will take you in immediately, she also told me to get up and get out of the house and spend the night some where else, because the police could come through the night and take my girls from me, so when I got off the phone with her, I didn't even pack, I just left; but God came through for me again, he got nothing that he took me to court for. Thank You Jesus! [remembering back when we first went to court, getting our divorce he told the judge that I was obese, my mother was obese, and her whole family, and he said that we didn't believe in education, all we believed in was church. The judge stopped him and said wait a minute Mr. Sir, now you married her, and I'm not going to sit here and let you speak like this about her and leave her family out of this, its between you and her.]

As the girls got older, they started accepting visitations a little better they were now at the ages of four and eight. MDT got even serious, and so did the questions, but every time they had a question, I prayed to give the best and truthful answer I could, even when I had to tell the truth on myself; and no matter how many times they asked or kept wanting to know something, I was there and they in return would go back to their daddy asking if what I had told them was the truth, and every time he would tell them that I was wrong. This brought about confusion to them, especially to Xenia, she even told me herself, but all I could say to her was, Xenia, mommy is telling you the truth, I have no reason to lie to you; first of all your mother has a fear of God, and hell is real and

I'm not going for you, Aarion or nobody else, so all I can say to you now is, ask God, and he will show you the truth in time. I brought them to court on one of the times among many, but this time I wanted the judge to talk to the girls, and hear their side of the story; why they didn't like visitation with their daddy, but the judge refused to see them; all he thought was that me and my love was being childish and blaming each other for the mess we created, but I argued every time; trying to let the judge see that I wasn't blaming anyone nor was I being childish; I didn't think that the girls should have been forced to do something they did not want to do, because I saw the trauma that it took them through as well as myself, I really disliked that judge; because he wasn't seeing things from a child's stand point, nor did he live with us, and if you're not on the inside, you only know the outside view.

The judge even asked me what if the shoe was on the other foot. I said to him, I've already thought about that, and only God knows that I would be hurt, but if my girls didn't want to be with me, then for the sake of their happiness, and well being, I would stay away; although I would be dying on the inside, I would have to respect their wishes. Yes, children are to be respected, they are people with feelings, and thoughts of their own. I just thought that the judge didn't care about my girls feelings. So when we came out from the judges chambers my daughters asked, is the judge going to see us mommy. I told them no, they wanted to know why; all the way there, they were saying what they were going to say to the judge, like why they didn't like going over to their daddy's house, but if no one wants to hear their voice in the matter, then they felt like they didn't matter, and that's what Xenia asked me, doesn't what we have to say, or how we feel count? I told her to me it does.

Me being the mother, thought of an idea of having a family meeting with my love, his mother, myself, my mother and the girls, the thing I wanted to accomplish was for them (he and his mother) to really hear the girls out, and see their point; but it didn't work, the meeting ended with me getting hurt, and the girls even more confused. I left the house and left my girls with my mother, and I went for a drive; but yet the visitations continued, and so did the crying. With all this going back and forth to the courthouse, and watching my girls go through changes, my hair fell out, my weight went up and down, as well as my emotions, my health was failing, and yet I had to go on trying to be strong for me and my girls. The thing that had me hurting from the meeting was, when my love said that Xenia had told him that she wanted to live with him when she turned twelve, and when we asked Aarion who she wanted to live with she said, she didn't care who she lived with as long as that parent bought her some golden arch French fries everyday. They were five and nine at the time of the meeting, but anyway I found out later the real truth. Xenia said to me that when she turned twelve that she would be taken from me.

But God brought everything to a screeching halt. Be careful what you pray for, for God always answers your prayers; and it may not be the way you think. You can read the conclusions of all these matters in Xenia's Flight.

CHAPTER TWO

Xenia's Flight

On Our Own

Well here we are finally in our own place; October 1998, 1202 Shannon Chase Drive, Union City, GA. It was here where I really started trusting God; after talking to one of Xenia's god parents Pastor K. P., he said to me during a phone conversation, Shun, I know that you've been on your own now for a while with your girls, but now you need to trust God even the more, and then he said to me, Shun trust is a spirit; so pray and ask God for the spirit of trust, and I did. I started praying, Lord I trust you with my life, and in every area of my life. We were so happy; now we were free to walk around the way we wanted to, and just be girlfriends, chillin. We had so much fun with each other; hanging out at the movies, going out to eat at our favorite place, Houston's; sometimes it would be just the three of us, and other times it would be the whole family. I tried to make beautiful memories with my daughters, thinking that I would be the one to go first, and if so, they would say our mother really left us something to hold on too. One trip we took, was to Chattanooga, TN. to see Ruby Falls, and to see Rock City, Lookout Mountain, and the Incline, boy did we have lots of fun; we got there a day early, checked into a hotel so that the next day we would be ready for our long walk, and boy was it ever, Xenia was tired of all the walking we had to do, she reminded me of myself, people use to call her my twin. Sometimes around 1:00 a.m.

Or 2:00 a.m. we would get up out of the bed because we couldn't sleep, and ride to down town Atlanta and look at the lights, or ride through Buck head looking at the big mansions, saying how one day we would live there, or we'd go to auntie Phyllis when she lived in Peachtree City, waking her up; she'd come to the door saying what are ya'll doing up this time of morning? But she'd let us on in with our night clothes on and goodies from the grocery store, they'd watch movies and we'd play scrabble.

Another trip we took was to Alabama, where I had to sing and I called them up to sing with me, the crowd loved it; and so did they, trying to be shy. I took my girls on as many trips that I could, another trip was to New Orleans, to the Jazz festival where I was the gospel artist on the ticket, more fun; now my girls and I, we are the hotel room service queens, nobody in the world loves room service like we do, our bill would sometimes be well over $ 150.00 and I wouldn't mind not one bit; these were my babies; and as I said before, if God blessed me with money, and they wanted it, they got it; they were poor little rich girls, but I didn't let them know. Yes, there were times when mommy just didn't have it, and I'd let them know that if God wanted us to have it then he would provide it. Xenia's birthday was coming up and she wanted to be picked up at school in a Limousine and I just didn't have it, but I called her Uncle J. and her grandmother and they got her that Limousine, I couldn't pay enough money, nor give enough Thanks for the smile I saw, and the scream I heard; when we pulled up in that car at her school, I got out holding a sign which read HAPPY BIRTHDAY XENIA! WE LOVE YOU. I also tried to instill in them about paying tithes, and giving offerings no matter what, don't steal God's money; I would say to them the reason we don't steal God's money is because we don't want to be cursed, we want to be blessed(Malachi,3:8-12). My girls would do all the grocery shopping I had to do, of course after me taking them with me for a while; Xenia caught on very fast, so the next time I needed to go to the store, she said I'll go in mommy; you just sit right here until I get back, she would use these same words as she went into the Post Office to get money orders to pay the bills, and I would do as she had instructed me. When ever Xenia went shopping; and she got to the register; she would say to Aarion;

Aarion, I got a feeling we're gonna need some more money, and Aarion would ask how much; and Xenia would tell her how much to ask for, and out the store Aarion would come yelling; Xenia said she thinks we gone need some more money, I would say how much more, then she would say umm, about twenty dollars; I'd give her the money, she'd take it back and out the store they would come, it seem like every time they went shopping Xenia had a "feeling". One time I just didn't have a lot of money; and I told her to get only what was on the list, well she went in, but after awhile; here come Aarion running to the car saying mama Xenia got that feeling again; I told her to tell Xenia that I had a feeling she needed to put something back; cause I don't have anymore money; the thing was, they would be trying to surprise me with something or Xenia would be trying to buy a cookbook, and she'd come out of the store with that long face and I would have to explain to her all over again about us not having enough money at that time. Arriving at home, I would pull the car around to the back side of the apartment, right up to our door, and we'd unload the van, and afterwards, I'd take the car back around to the front, then we would put away the groceries, and Xenia would cook dinner; she would again instruct me to go in the room, relax and watch TV and she would bring my plate to me and something to drink; Xenia would cook sautéed shrimp, steaks, Swedish meatballs, green eggs and Spam with cheese. Whenever I was home, that girl would spoil me so, and I know it was because my mother would tell them, this is you all's mother and you should take care of her, for all the things she do for you; going out there on the road preaching and singing, trying to make ends meet, and keep a roof over your heads and etc...I know because I heard her tell them this several times. Because just like children, they would get a little ungrateful at times, when I couldn't do for them like I wanted to; it seemed like they didn't understand; and right then and there my mother would say to them, now I know I don't see the faces I'm seeing; she would say to them how they should act, and boy they did not like for grand mommy to get on them, Xenia would just cry and cry saying I'm sorry mommy and Aarion would follow, and I would forgive them as always. Xenia was the type of child that would do anything for her mommy, her sister, and her family, she was a daddy's girl; who loved her mommy; what I mean by this is, she loves her daddy a lot, but she'd rather stay with her mother, and Aarion is a mommies girls, who loves her daddy; but still wants to stay with mommy. Xenia called me Mommy, and Aarion calls me Mama.

The Warning Signs

Xenia hated school with a passion, because the children at school would pick at her and call her names, this happened from the time she started private school until middle school; grades kindergarten through six grade. Everyday she came home from school, she would say mommy this person said this about me, or that person did this to me, one day after (elementary) school Xenia got in the car crying, and holding her throat. I was immediately mad and upset and didn't know why, all I knew was that somebody had said something to her again, so I asked her what was the matter? She could barely talk to me, saying that two girls ganged up on her in the hallway, and one of them choked her and they both were saying threatening things to her; and that she was scared. When I say everyday it literally was everyday; she would ask me to let her stay home and miss school, then I would say girl your daddy is already trying to take you from me, and if I allow you to stay home the judge would take you from me and give you to him, with no questions asked. They were tired of visitations; Xenia was sitting on the bed and out from no where she said I HATE! my daddy. I heard her from the inside, and I saw the look on her face, I then turned around to her and asked her what brought that on? and she said I hate what he did to you, I told her that she could not get into heaven feeling that way, no matter what; she had to forgive him just like I did. We talked a little bit more at MDT (Mother and daughter time). I saw a whole new spirit trying to take over Xenia, I told my mother about it and we took it in prayer. One night lying in the bed praying, I saw this black mass come up from Xenia's body, from where she was laying and floated out of the window, I just began to praise God, because I knew that what I had seen earlier, God took it away. Thank You Jesus!

Another time she was cooking and walked to the bedroom door and just stood there, she would look at me and then look at the floor, like she was thinking about something, so I said what's wrong Xenia? She said to me, there's a spirit that's being passed down through all the girls in my classroom, and I asked what spirit? Then she said a lesbian spirit; and we talked, she said to me that sometimes she would have thoughts of being with a girl, and I told her that the devil will always bring evil, bad no good thoughts to our minds, but where we go wrong is when we give in to those thoughts. I told her that having thoughts of lesbianism doesn't make you one, ask God to forgive you of those thoughts and go on and if you need more help and feel like you can't do it, we will fast and pray together and get grand mommy to fast and pray with us too, but before she went back to the kitchen I said lets pray now Xenia; we prayed and asked God to forgive us and told him how much we loved him and we hugged each other, she looked at me and said mommy I thank God for you, I feel so much better. Now all their lives when I prayed for them, or over them during my prayer time in the morning was, Lord, before anybody tried to hurt them or bring harm or danger to them, Lord you take those persons out of this world; little did I know that he had another plan in mind. One day my girls wanted to talk to me (MDT) about one of their visitation weekends, Xenia stressed to me that she didn't like the way her daddy would touch her on her thigh when he would wake her up, or play with her, so I told her to tell him, he is your daddy and you can tell him how you feel. Just say daddy, I don't like it when you do this, that and the other; but Xenia didn't like to hurt anyone, if she thought it was going to bring confrontation of any kind, she wouldn't' do it or say it. Xenia was the old me and Aarion is the new me.

I remember Xenia saying to Aarion concerning their daddy,

because she (Aarion) hated visitations, so she would say things that she didn't like about him, and Xenia would say Aarion don't say that because he's hurting too, we have to pray for him. I'm not trying to make myself look good, because there were times I hated him and everybody that I thought were trying to hurt my girls, but in spite of how I felt, I NEVER! taught my girls to hate their daddy; I always told them to love him, no matter what, because when it's all said and done, he's still your daddy. I kept telling them to do the right things until God did the work in me, and on me; and I'm glad to say today that God did the complete work. I forgave my love for everything that happened and I called him up and asked him to forgive me, not if I had done anything, but for what I had done; just like it takes two to make a baby, it takes two to make a marriage and this is just Shun's belief, that it takes two to break a marriage.

One day Xenia got in the car from me picking her up at school and she had encountered a real bad day, she was in middle school at this time and some of the girls had treated her funny, and she just couldn't understand why people would treat other people so badly. Xenia had a heart of pure gold, never brought harm to anyone all she had to give was love; case and point, the school chorus had a party and Xenia begged me if she could buy cupcakes and sodas for the entire class and she did; second case, the day of Valentine, seven days before her death; once again Xenia begged me the night before, and the day of, if she could buy valentine cards and candy for over sixty students at her school. Sitting in the parking lot of the store, she was almost late for school signing cards and filling them with candy and after getting to school we had yet to finish more cards, and after passing them out to the students that day, picking her up from school she was crying, I asked what was wrong? And she said mommy, you know all those cards I gave to the students, I saw them later on that day in trash cans. This is why I know my daughter Xenia did not die of a heart attack, but from the attacks to her heart. Anyway moving on, she brought the conversation up again about letting her stay out of school. So while leaving dinner later that night, I said to them girls tonight we are going to have a very serious MD Time, especially for you Xenia, alright? They said, yes mam mommy, but they started asking, are we in trouble or something? I smiled and said no, but it will be serious. So night came and there we were on the bed in a circle, I started the conversation this time saying to Xenia you have stressed to me how much you hate school; now the only way that you don't go back to school is that God send us enough money to hire a private tutor, or send that RICH husband, or you die and go home to be with the Lord, these are the only reasons that you could never go back to school, now if you are ready to go be with the Lord; let me know and I in return will go to your grandmother (my mother) and tell her, and we'd go to God on your behalf, now which one is it? Then I said to her don't answer me right away because I want you to think about your answer. She sat there for a while like she was really thinking about what I had just said, and she waited, finally she, said I want to stay with you mommy; then I said alright then, you've got to go to school. As a mother, I tried with all that was within me to build her up, telling her how beautiful she was and that the other girls were hating on her with her long black hair and sassy walk given by God, without even trying Xenia had a twist naturally like her great-grandmother, my mother and me, then she had a slight bounce as she walked, just gorgeous, beautiful inside and out, no she wasn't skinny, but she was shapely just like her momma, ME! I tell people when I'm up ministering don't call me fat; just call me blessed; and I'm blessed in all the right places. I wanted Xenia to have the esteem that God had given me, but it seemed like all the talking I did, was no good.

As long as she was at home with me; she was alright, but as soon as she went to school; some no good, evil, ugly, hatred, no mannered, unlearned, ignorant, trifling, player hating "n's" would tare down everything I tried to build up. I could see the hurt in her eyes, I could see the pain, but there was nothing I could do, only God.

About three years leading up to Xenia's death I had a dream, in the dream we had been in an accident, but there was no blood no where, and there was a man dressed in all white, it looked like a doctors outfit, the coat was long just below the knee and I saw his pants. He was carrying Xenia, she looked lifeless, her arms were just hanging and she had on white, a beautiful laced collard dress, and while he was walking towards me he was saying to me; you are a good mother, you have been a real good mother, I shared the dream with my mother, but she didn't say anything until later on, she said that she started praying against accidents and Xenia getting hurt. Me, I thought that God was easing my mind because I have always had the question in the back of my mind, Lord I wonder if I'm a good mother? Because I traveled all the time, but when I got back home, I tried to make up for "being away time", the Lord reminded me of this dream a year later after her death. One day I was laying in my prayer room, with my eyes closed; I saw a vision of fiery darts coming towards me from the apartment across the way. I took it to be on the look out for my neighbor, to not like me or something, not knowing that the fiery trails ahead would be in the area of finance, no engagements coming in, or going out (smile), the death of my first born; and many other trails, but the Lord, delivered me out of them all. [Psalms 34:19]. I remember my god parents coming over for dinner and before they left, I asked if he would pray over me, my girls and our place of living.

He prayed for God's protection; and then said, just like in the days of Moses, when the Lord said: when I see the blood; I will pass over thee: I began to cry, because those were the exact words I prayed one day after we had just moved in, and I was outside anointing the house with oil, speaking those words as I was praying, so you see she couldn't have died there, because God had to honor his word. The man of god also spoke the word of the Lord which said because thou art mine, I will do this for you and I will do that for you, because you belong to me said God: even then God knew what was going to take place; so hearing the words, that I belonged to him; gave me great comfort knowing that I was in the hands of the Almighty God. As I am known for saying, The God of Abraham, The God of Isaac, The God of Jacob and The God of LaShun Pace.

About a month before the Lord took Xenia she would ask me mommy do you think I would be as famous as you one day, I told her yes, even greater; then she kept asking me from time to time if I loved her, almost everyday twice a day she would ask me this question, Mommy do you love me? Until one night she asked me again, if I loved her and it kind of made me upset, so I stopped everything

I was doing, to assure her of how much I really loved her. I in return asked her a question, Xenia, do you know the hell I went through with your daddy and the divorce? She said yes mam, I said to her, if I had to go through "alllll" of that again, knowing that I would come out with You and Aarion, I would do it again. She then said to me, you love me that much? I said that plus, and then some, she smiled so big and said, Thank You mommy, you make me feel so good, we hugged each other and sealed it with a kiss.

The Day She Made Me Sing

I was in the studio working on my last project with my record company "the last word in gospel music" at a studio in Conyers, Georgia; which from where I lived was about a thirty-five or forty minute ride one way depending upon the trafic, we had been working now for about three months. One day we were laying music tracks and I was doing scratch vocals, my sister Leslie was with me and noticed my hands balled up very tight and she said Shun, what's wrong why are you so tensed? I said I don't know, well weeks went by and we had finished with all the musical tracks, now we were laying down my lead vocals and background vocals. I would let them come on Fridays and Saturday to watch mommy working it out in the studio (smile), maybe once or twice on a Monday because this was family nights for us, we would call each others house by their address, we'd say okay, who's house we're at this Monday, fifty two fifty, thirty two ninety or whatever the address was. We are very tight and close knit family, my friend in Texas, ace "T" call us the Christian mafia Family; mess with us; we'll call on the big three (Father, Son & Holy Ghost) along with Michael, Gabriel, Sinclair and Raphael and a host of others. Anyway moving on, I don't know exactly when this feeling came over me but I started feeling death all around me every day for about two weeks or so before her death and I couldn't shake it, I started rebuking it, but it wouldn't leave, I thought it was me because it was so strong. One night at the studio, Xenia and Aarion was there and there was a song I was going to do with them but not this particular week, but something said no go ahead and do it now while they are her (not really knowing that it was God at work) so I glanced out the window and I saw Xenia going up the hall, I had told them to go to the car because we were getting ready to leave. I had just finished my last song for the night, I told somebody; I don't know who it was, but I said stop Xenia and Aarion; tell them to come back, lets do this song right quick. I was thinking lets do this one and it will be another song out the way, plus it was a very short song, just us and the piano and later we'd add more stuff if we wanted to. And so we did the song, me and my girls, "A Mother's Prayer". The song came from a play I was in. And in the play there was a scene where I was encouraging a little girl about her family, but we didn't have a song; so the director asked me if I could write something that would fit and the Lord gave me the words and the melody, I song it to him and he loved it.

It's about eight days before her death. Xenia had volunteered me to sing at her school for Black History week, she got up one morning and said mommy I told the school that you would sing for black history on Thursday around one o'clock p.m., well before I would sing, I had to go back out to the studio and finish up, and get my big little check, so I went, we finished the song I had to do, and cleaned up a few tracks vocally and musically, now I was just waiting on my turn to be called in the room to receive my check, but my turn never came, and the money man was getting ready to leave; so I first went to my M.D., and asked, so what's up with my check? Because he had the payroll, he then said to me that my check wasn't there, that I had to get mine from the head company. I said WHAT! What kind of mess is this? They knew I had to be paid three months ago, and now that I'm through they can't pay me. I was told later that the company didn't know if I was going to give them a good project, or just throw some congregational songs together and let it go at that.

I told them first of all I don't sing for them; I sing for the glory of God; and I ain't gone give God no junk and anyway if I did do a bunch of congregational songs you can bet your life that they would have been anointed; and I would have given it my all, needless to say I left the studio very upset, this company has always done me wrong, and I was feed up, they made me so mad until I didn't even want to sing at my daughter's school, in fact I told my sister to take me home. How could he come all the way here and not bring my money; after all it was mine, I had worked for every dime. So while riding in the car on our way back home I began to cry, Durancice was driving and my friend R. C., was with us; my sister started praying and calling on the name of Jesus, and she began to prophecy under the leading of the Spirit of God, the Lord said that he was going to deal with the record company and the individuals involved, then he said, I'm going to show you this day how much I love you and what you mean to me; after she finished she said to me Shun, I think you need to reconsider about not going to Xenia's school, and so I did, I said to myself I'm not gonna let these folks keep me from making my daughter happy. Besides, Xenia had picked out what she wanted me to wear, it was a two piece black sweater like material outfit with boots to match, I wasn't going to change because I was so upset and I just didn't feel like changing, then I thought about the outfit that Xenia had picked out for me to wear and I told my sister to take me by the house and let me change, so we stopped by the house, I only had enough time to change and get to the school, when I got there they were waiting for me, and when they called my name the students went crazy, they started yelling, screaming, stumping and beating on the bleachers, there I was standing in the middle of the gymnasium holding the mike saying ya'll quiet down; but they would not settle down, the coach was blowing his whistle, the teachers were waving their hands trying to calm them down, then I said okay ya'll I'm not going to sing until you be quiet, then they stopped a little, so I announced the song that I would be singing "I know I've been changed" and they started all over again screaming YEA! And after they settled down again, that's when I told them, that I was there for only one reason and that reason was my daughter. (I was pointing in her direction, she was standing against the wall at the back of the gym with this big smile on her face) Xenia Pace Rhodes. And when I finished singing Xenia came from off the wall out to where I was with her arms stretched out as wide as she could get them, her head tilted with this great big I'm so pleased smile and (for a few seconds I felt like we switched rolls, I felt like I was her daughter, and she was my mother) she gave me the biggest hug and I griped her right back, she said Thank You mommy, I love you, and I said I love you too baby, with all my heart, and as usual while we were hugging each other, she said mommy can I leave school early? And I said, of course baby, her face lit up with a big smile and she thanked me again.

On my way out of the auditorium one of the students ran to me for an autograph and the next thing I knew I was being mobbed by students wanting me to sign their papers and take pictures. I felt like a real star, the incident that had happened earlier at the studio I didn't even remember, it didn't matter anymore. So when I got to the car my sister said to me didn't the Lord say that he was going to show you how much he loved you and what you mean to him? With tears in my eyes I said, Yes he did! I then got out of the car and went prostrate on the ground in my black two piece outfit to give him thanks. I have a gift from God, to hear death bells, and one day I had heard a lot of them, more than the norm in one day, so going to bed that night, we all were settled in, and while laying there I heard another bell, and I said sharply God! And both girls at the same time said what's wrong mommy/mama? I said, if I hear another death bell…Xenia, while laying down with her back towards me, rose up a little, turned her head slightly towards me and asked, was one of them for me mommy? Ya'll should have heard me, I told her NO! I was calling the devil all kinds of liars, lies he ain't even told yet, I was rebuking the devil, quoting scriptures pleading the blood of Jesus, and everything.

It's Tuesday, February 20th, yet dealing with that death feeling. I had picked Aarion up from school, and Duranice had got Demarcus, we met at the school together; and the Principal, came out to the car to make sure we'd be at P.T.A. that night and that they would be serving homemade chili, I said alright, if the Lord's will we would be there. But I've NEVER! liked PTA meetings, every since I was a little girl; all through school, because it seemed like I got a whipping after every meeting, and I vowed to myself that if I had children, I would never go to a PTA, especially if it made them feel like I did, all scared and nervous in the stomach, yuck! Three times, M. H. (smile), so teachers this is why you never see me at PTA. Anyway after leaving their school we got Xenia, and on our way home, I asked the girls which did they want to do, go to PTA, or go to the movies? Xenia said um! The movies. So I got the attention of my sister and we pulled over into the parking lot of a grocery store and I told her that they wanted to go to the movies instead of PTA. We went home freshened up, changed clothes and headed out for the movies, at greenbrier mall. It was there when I told my sister Duranice about the death feelings I was having, I told her that I feel like its me who's going to die because it was so, so, so, so, strong, the only way I can describe it is; I felt like it was a blanket that had wrapped me up and I couldn't get out or take if off, and just like I did when Xenia asked was one of the death bells for her, when I told Duranice of the death feeling, she starting rebuking death and telling the devil he was a lair and that I shall live and not die. I felt a little better but the feeling of death stayed. We saw an Evangelist friend of my sister that night at the movies, and we began to share some things with her, and she prayed also, but the feeling would not leave. My sister and I had watched a movie and upon leaving that particular theatre I had this freaky fall, I know I saw the steps but I missed all three of them; trying to hold on to the rail and missed that too, it was like slow motion and the way I landed, I should have broke my neck, or a leg, but instead I had these bad bruises on my thigh, my leg, and my neck was really sore, all I heard was my sister calling my name, Shun! Oh my God! Are you alright? I was shaking all over, when I got up that's when I told her that something was wrong and I felt like something bad was going to happen. I told her of how I'd been feeling death all around me, this time she was quiet, maybe she was thinking the same thing that I was thinking. When we got together with the children, we called down to Florida to let them speak to Phyllis "auntie mommy".

Because the next morning she was scheduled for surgery, so we called to let them say hello and that she's going down with angels and getting up with angels. Xenia talked to her and told her that she loved her, that was all she could say because Aarion grabbed the phone away yelling I love you too auntie Phyllis, I can't get the look out of my head that was on Xenia's face when Aarion grabbed the phone from her, it was like she was cut off from something, then it changed to a well, that's alright kinda look. We all spoke to her and then said goodbye, that's when Duranice and I looked at each other saying you think it may be Phyllis? There we started again rebuking the devil and pleading the blood of Jesus. Well one thing we knew, nobody was dying that night, because we had rebuked enough devils, prayed enough prayers and pleaded buckets of the blood of Jesus.

The movie that Xenia wanted to see was "Save the last dance" after the movies we went to my brother's house, there we ate, played scrabble, and watched more movies on cable TV. After Xenia finished eating she went to the sofa, laid back and said, mommy my heart hurts, with the look that I saw, I immediately said, "I rebuke death in the name of Jesus" (there was a glow about her face) I wasn't afraid of that but it was the words "my heart hurts" that got my attention. Other times through the years she would say mommy my heart is beating funny, but like I said prior, I didn't worry over it because I suffer with irregular heart beat, so I thought this was happening to her, so I said to her, Xenia you know how you would go and sit on the floor against the wall at home for awhile? She said yes mam, I said try doing that and see if you don't feel better, yes mam she said. She did, and the next thing I knew, she was stretched out on the floor sleep. Duranice and I continued to play scrabble, until I noticed the time, (almost 12:00 a.m.) I said girl we got to go, school is tomorrow, and they already don't wanna go, so we got them up calling their names, when Xenia got up, she leaned on the arm of the loveseat where I was, looking at me saying (like an old woman) "whew" that nap did me a world of good, we just laughed and I said, how do you feel now Xenia? She said I feel real good mama (the first time she ever said mama), then I said well Thank you Jesus! We got in the car and headed for home. While riding home, Xenia was leaning on the window looking up towards the sky, then she said "mommy I had a really good time tonight" I said I'm glad baby, she got quiet for a while and then said "mommy I sure do miss Dee Dee (not her real name, who passed away three years earlier).

Then she said a little while later, I sure do miss my god daddy (who passed away nine months earlier), I looked back at her, wondering why is she thinking about people who were gone? But I said, I miss them too baby. Then for no special reason, I called my boyfriend's mother, we talked with her, said our "we love you" and hung up. I don't know why, but this old song dropped in my spirit and I started singing, "I know the Lord, will make away, Oh yes he will", when Xenia joined right in, singing along with me. It touched my heart because I didn't know she knew that song, it was way before her time, so I asked her how did she know that song? She said they sang it at her daddy's church.

After getting home, we all prepared for going to bed and went to sleep, when I was awakened by this hideous cough from Xenia, which hit me smack dab in the middle of my stomach, (it was about four something that morning) I jumped up looking at her to see if she was alright, she began to move slowly raising up, sitting on the side of the bed, then she went to the bathroom, I just laid there troubled in my spirit, she was in there so long I drifted back off to sleep, but I woke up noticing she was yet in there, so I said to my self if she stay in there any longer I'm going in there after her, soon as I said that I heard her coming out, I quickly laid back down like I was sleep. Now, when ever Xenia got up through the night like that and came back to bed, she would touch me and say, are you alright mommy, or something, she would do this without fail. But this time when she got back into bed she said NOTHING to me, or touched me, she did nothing at all. I then frowned and said, "this girl aint said nothing to me, what's up with this? But now I know that it was the Lord who wouldn't let me say a word.

It's seven on the nose, every morning like clock work, unless we were tired, I would get them up, "Xenia, Aarion" time to get up girls, and like every morning, Xenia would give this crying sigh and say "Oh Jesus" but this time after saying it, sitting on the side of the bed, her head down, all sad with tears in her eyes, all at once she gave this slight jump, perked up as if some one said to her, you can do it, it's the last time you'll ever do this again, she started getting ready like she was on a mission, talking only to her sister, and saying nothing to me. I continued my routine, shouting "come on girls, hurry up and get dress, brush your teeth, comb your hair, do this that and the other, I didn't get you up on time to be late, usually we would put on our armour and pray, but that morning I was rushing them, and I was upset because they started moving slow, so I left them in the house, telling them I'll see yall in the car and don't forget to lock up. Here they come looking like, I don't wanna go to school, we had prayer in the car, I dropped Aarion off first, did our hugs and kisses and my three toots on the car horn, now on my way to take Xenia to her school, because of my mother, Xenia would every morning, stop off at J's restaurant for breakfast and while sitting in front of her school she would finish eating, until it was time for her to go into the building, this particular morning I didn't have enough money for her to stop off at her place for breakfast, she slightly looked over to where the restaurant was, saying nothing all the way to school.

Well here we are sitting at her school, not really saying nothing to each other, I know on my mind was the speaking engagement I had that Saturday I had been studying on what I was going to say, it was a youth convention. We were listening to the radio, she loved music, anyway I said alright Xenia it's time for mommy to go, I have to get back home to finish studying for this weekend, she gave a sigh and said yes ma'am mommy, she motioned like she was opening the door, but never did. She sat back on the seat, she did not want to get out of the car, I said Okay Xenia, she then asked me if I could pull down a little further to let her out on the gravel instead of the dirt part, I did as she requested, but she kept sitting there, then I said, get out Xenia and get into that school, then we hugged and kissed each other as always and said our, "I love yous", she got out, open the back door to get her book bag, saying to me, mommy you don't have to pick me up until four o'clock because of chorus rehearsal that evening, I said okay baby, I'll see you this evening if the Lord's will, she shut the door, walked on the gravel a little ways, turned to me and started waving bye, I waved back and proceeded to drive off doing my three toots (I love you). Driving off slowly I noticed her in my rearview mirror yet standing there waving her right hand from side to side with no smile on her face, she was solemn, with a frown on my forehead, I almost stopped (not upset, just puzzled) saying within my self, why is this girl still standing there? So I tooted three more times, waving. Continuing on just before I was to turn the curve, I noticed her yet standing there waving, this time I hit the horn once, with my index finger pointing, saying get into that school, I said out, she's never done this before, why wont she go in the building? By this time I was out of sight, I stopped the car, looked down, and up again, turned back towards her direction, saying to my self, now if I went back right now Xenia would jump in this car and go home with me happy, but Lord you know I can't do that, (in my mind I said, I'm going through enough already, I don't need nobody saying I'm keeping my children out of school for no apparent reason) so I went on home. I didn't know that within about thirty minutes or so, that my whole world was about to be turned up side down. If anyone would have told me that, that would be the last time I would see my baby, the school would not have seen her that day. But I had told God that I TRUSTED HIM!

But I trusted in thee, O Lord: I said, thou art my God.
(Ps. 31:14, 15a)
My times are in thy hand:

XENIA'S FLIGHT

I had just dropped her off at school, came back home took the phone off the hook, laid across the bed and began to study the word of God, preparing a sermon the Lord gave me to speak at the conference in Rochester, New York. This was Wednesday morning Feb. 21, 01. I was to leave Friday coming. While laying on the bed, suddenly I heard a banging at my bedroom window, it was June my sister saying, the school just called and said that Xenia had fallen out and lost consciousness, the first thing that came out of my mouth was **"THE BLOOD OF JESUS!"** little did I know, that the moment I spoke those words, God sealed me with a supernatural protection.

I got dressed in less than a minute and out the door, getting ready to get into my car, my sister said no, ride with me, I'll take you. Off we went speeding, heading towards the school, by the time we got to the traffic light, under the bridge, an ambulance came flying pass us, from the direction of her school, I said June that's her, there we went chasing behind the ambulance, going through lights, stop signs and all, until this police car came flying behind us flagging us down, when he caught up with us, he was trying to tell us to stop and slow down, and I was trying to tell him that, that's my baby in that ambulance ahead of us, he made us pull over and when he did, June broke down, like she had lost something. The police didn't give us a ticket, he said that he understood, but we could get hurt and hurt some one else, he said I'm not telling y'all to not follow the ambulance, but you must acknowledge the traffic lights and stop signs, he told us what hospital they were going to and to slow down because we were going too fast, I apologized and we went on.

We got to the hospital, while walking towards the door, I called my manager/boyfriend and left him a message about what had happened, and that I would keep him informed about what was going on, told him I love him and hung up. I'm inside and the first person I see is her daddy, with this angry look, but I wasn't there for him, my attitude was, where is my baby and is she alright. What happened? What made her fall out? At this time the school nurse saw me, took me to this little room, there was a end table two double love seated chairs and two single chairs, it was me, my love, his mother, my sister and another lady who I didn't know, she was sitting to the left of me, her nose was very red, she was rocking back and forward,

With her hands up to her face, so I asked her what was wrong? Her response was, "We need God now". Judging from her looks and the way she made that statement, I knew that something was very wrong, (the lady was the school principal) the nurse kept coming in and out of the room checking on us to see if we were alright, then she would say from time to time, that they are doing all they can. I'm looking at the nurse with a look like, okay, then I said thank you very much, then my love looked over to me and said, "Shun can I see you for a moment?" I said, "Sure". We went out to the lobby of the hospital, he then begin to ask me questions about Xenia, which started to up set me, so I said to him this is not the time nor the place; trying to blame me or anybody else, then he asked if I had insurance and if I didn't that he would take care of everything. I politely said, "Thank you" and went back into the little waiting room and sat down, I began to sing, I don't know why because singing was the furthest thing from my mind. But a force deep down inside of me began to wail on the inside. I felt something in my belly and the song just flowed out of my mouth, [I will trust in the Lord, I will trust in the Lord, I will trust in the Lord (now the original words that go here is, "till I die") but the Spirit of God had my tongue, and all I could say was, "**AT ALL TIMES**". He knew what was ahead, because I had no clue. So I kept singing and when I finished, I heard the Lord say to me, "What would your mother do if she was here?" I said, "She would start praying." So I got on my knees in that little room, not caring who heard me and I started praying for the doctors, that God would give them what to do concerning Xenia, Lord direct their hands, Lord what ever is wrong, fix it; Jesus. While I was praying, I heard the voice of the Lord speak to me again, this time he said to me, "where are you? Look at where you are." I said, "a hospital," then he said to me, "some one else is worse off than you, start praying for somebody else." And in obedience I quickly began praying, "Lord go up and down these hospital halls, touch and heal some body, Holy Spirit go to the ICU floor, and give some one a miracle, somebody need a miracle." After praying, I got back up and sat down. Then I began to groan in the spirit, then every one came back into the room, along with the hospital nurse, the doctor and the school nurse, they all sat down except for the school nurse, the doctor began to ask us some questions about Xenia's heart, if she had ever had heart problems, and I said, "no sir, except for last night," then he asked what happened last night?

So I told him and he asked was that the only time and I said, "well at times she would say to me that her heart was flooding, which I didn't worry about, because I have that same thing, it only happens when I'd drink sodas or eat chocolate or it would happen for no reason at all. The doctor just looked, so sitting there I thought that he was going to tell us that Xenia needed to rest, or ya'll take her home and let her stay in bed for a month or two, or something along those lines. But on his face he was troubled and puzzled at the same time, and I was looking like, "WHAT!' What is it? Just tell us, then he said with a sigh, we've tried everything, we've done all that we could do, then that's when my love burst out saying, "so what are you saying? What are you telling me? Is my child dead?' All while I'm watching the doctor, I saw his head drop to his chest nodding yes. My love began screaming, kicking, swinging his arms back and forth and hollering, "NO! NO! NO! Not my child. Then he ran out the room and fell on to the floor. My sister, June took off running, but she didn't make it past the door when she fell to the floor yelling, "NO! It can't be." Then she got up asking, "is this a dream? I'm dreaming this can't be real." Me, I was still in the room, I know I was sitting down, but some how without fainting, I lost consciousness, and my mind went blank. If you ask me how I went from sitting down to standing up with my hands in the prayer position, to my mouth, I couldn't tell you. All I could do was say over and over again, "my baby is dead, my baby is dead, MY BABY IS DEAD." My knees felt like jelly, like they were going to give any moment. Then all of a sudden I had this urge to walk, so I left the room and was headed out of the hospital when I heard a voice say, "Go to Xenia." I turned around and there was a nurse, I asked her if I may see my daughter, she said, "no," when I turned from her there was another nurse, I asked her the same question, "can I please see my baby?" and she said, "yes, follow me." While I was walking with her I was praying now Lord you told me to go to Xenia, are you going to raise her up or what? Then I said, "well Lord whatever it is I'm going and what ever you want me to do I'm here." By this time the nurse pulled me back by my arm and said, "now, I need to prepare you before you go in(behind the curtain), she has a tube in her mouth from where they were working on her," I said, "okay."

I can hear the sound of that curtains going back, when I saw her laying there, not moving at all, I walked over towards her looking at her, all the time saying in my head she's going to take a deep breath soon and say, "mommy." But that never happened, rubbing her face, talking to her, calling her name, hoping that she'd say something back; she never did. I began to cry, then I stopped because I believed God and I said, "If I cry he won't do it," so I dried my tears and looked up towards heaven and said, "God you got to talk to me, I need an angel to come through those curtain or appear on this wall." Then I looked at my baby and said, "Xenia, I can't release you until God speak to me and tell me something," and it wasn't long when the Lord whispered to me in my ear saying, "this was what she wanted." Then I started to cry asking her why didn't you tell me baby? Why didn't you tell mommy? Then the Lord said to me, "I have given her a glimpse into your future, and she's at peace." My Pastor walked in who was also Xenia's uncle, (Dennis L. Martin Sr.) I reached out to him for a hug, and I cried, while he hugged me I heard him take a deep sigh, he said something to me, but I can't remember what those words were. He stayed with me for a while and then went back to check on June. By this time a nurse walked in, she really wasn't doing anything, in fact after she left, I felt like she was an angel. She walked back and forth, and then she went on the other side of the bed facing me and said, "Are you going to have and autopsy done?" I said, "Mam, this is my first time being in this situation, I really don't know anything beside them taking her to the funeral home. Then she leaned over towards me and said, "If I were you, I would have an autopsy done, because they don't know why your baby died." When she said that it just gave me confirmation of what the Lord had told me when he said, "I took her, before she hit the ground. I took her; she didn't die of a heart attack." Then she said, "I'll go and get the papers and all you have to do is sign them. At first I didn't want an autopsy, because of what I had seen on TV, but I signed the papers and I'm glad I did. The media was hopping on her weight, saying that it was a heart attack. But when my sister Dejuaii went to the place where they were doing the autopsy(first of all she was going to raise her up in the name of Jesus), that's what she told us.

But upon walking on the grounds she said the Lord said to her, "what are you going to do?" she said, "to pray that you bring life back into her,' then she said the Lord spoke to her and said, "what if this is my will, and she don't want to come back," she said by this time some one was asking her how could they help her, she then asked if she could see Xenia. The person helping her said, "Ma'am, we are not suppose to do this and I could loose my job," but they took her to see Xenia any way. Dejuaii said when she saw her, she looked so peaceful. Dejuaii begin to ask questions and the person told her this child did not die from a heart attack, her heart muscles are not torn or stretched, the only thing we saw was that she had an enlarged heart and that a person could not die from that. Xenia's heart size was supposed to be around 200cm. but they said it was about 600cm. They also told her that usually adults only have enlarged hearts and that it came from deep depression and sadness.

I remember my mother telling me of a statement Xenia made to her; she said "grand mommy, life is so hard." Any way I'm so glad I signed those papers for the autopsy and I'm glad Dejuaii went to the coroners and received the information she did. Mean while back at the hospital, after signing the papers the nurse said that I had about an hour or so before the coroners came, and then she left. Sitting here holding Xenia's hand and kissing it, I began to speak in my heavenly language; no, not trying to bring her back, but just giving thanks to God for her life and the memories he had given me with her, then the Lord said to me, "I want you to see it this way, I chose you, and favored you, to be the Mother of a beautiful and sweet spirit. I began to cry and laugh at the same time, if nothing else, the Holy Spirit has taught me how to Praise God no matter what. My love would come in and out of the room from time to time. One time he came in while I was with Xenia, again I was speaking in my heavenly language just praising God, when he began to speak in a language unknown to me and God. I told my family what happened, and I said to them, (jokingly) "Xenia said, mommy I was coming back, but when she heard him, she said that's alright. Anyway I've learned how to tell God, Thank You. [**Thank God in everything no matter what the circumstances may be, be thankful and give thanks for this is the will of God for you who are in Christ Jesus the Revealer and Mediator of the will. (Amp. Version 1 Th. 5:18.)**

The coroners are here said the nurse, when they walked into the room to take my baby away that is when I broke down. Because another form of letting her go had come, if I could just keep looking at her, holding her hands, rubbing her hair, touching her cold body, I just did not want to let her go. I walked out of the room, as I was coming out they told me that my daughter Aarion had gotten there. Her daddy told her the news. It was told to me that he didn't take her to the side to tell it to her gently, he just came right out and said, "Your sister is dead." When they were bringing her to me, it was like she was in a trance, they had her by both arms leading her, when she saw me she fell on me crying saying, "mama Xenia's gone." Then she looked at me and said, "Can I see her mama? I want to see her," and I said, "Yes baby, you can see your sister." But when we got back there they had already taken her away. Oh the hurt I saw on Aarion's face, her buddy, her girlfriend and only sister; the one who taught her how to read and write her name, who went with her on her first day of school, like she was the mother, her movie partner. They could be in a store or a restaurant, hear music and would know what movie it was in and what was going on at the time the song was playing. They owned so many videos, they could have started a little rental store of their own.

If anything went wrong, Aarion would go to Xenia for advice. If I was upset, Xenia would tell Aarion how to handle me and what to do. They were tight just like my mother raised the ten of us to be. I tried my best to put the same wonderful things in my girls.

We left the hospital; I rode with Bishop W. who's known as "Mr. Clean", a friend and brother to my family, his wife and children as well. Soon as they got the news he and his wife(Mrs. G.W.) came to the hospital right away. Mr. C. had a chance to see my baby, he just hugged me tight. He took me home and even though he was trying to get me to go to his house so that I wouldn't have to be bothered with folk, I went to my Pastor's house. Sitting down stairs with Sister G.W. she was praying and interceding, my mother wasn't there, but God had her there for me. I don't know what happened, but all at once I screamed out, "NO! Lord NO!," and stumping my feet, when one foot came down on her feet.

I stopped and said, "I'm so sorry, please forgive me," and she said, "Girl please, it's okay you just lost a child," and she kept right on praying, calling on the name of Jesus. My mother was in Florida at the hospital with my sister Phyllis who was scheduled for surgery the same day. Thank you Sister G. I love you.

My Pastor and first Lady moved out of their bed for me and my daughter Aarion. They slept on the floor, but it was there at their house when God brought Xenia to me, I'm so thankful to them for how they surrounded us with a Godly atmosphere, June (my First Lady) who is my sister, turned to their twenty four hour gospel music satellite channel and never turned it off all while we were there (two weeks). Pastor would play some of his preaching tapes which was very up lifting, so when the spirit of grief tried to hit us, it couldn't stay because the presence of the Lord had moved into that place. I'm a living witness that if you **Praise God,** and **WORSHIP** Him grief, sadness, confusion, doubt, anger, bitterness, unforgiveness, old hurts and wounds, anxiety, thoughts of suicide, thoughts of hurting some one else (murder), hatred, jealousy, strife, envy and all other wrong thoughts or motives will **LEAVE!** Because when you praise God it sanctifies your atmosphere and brings peace, not just to your atmosphere, but peace in you. [May God himself, the God of peace, sanctify you through and through, may your whole spirit, soul and body be kept blameless at the coming of our Lord Jesus Christ, (New international version I Thessalonians 5:223)]

> [Thou wilt keep him in perfect peace, whose mind is stayed on thee: because he trusteth in thee. Trust ye in the Lord for ever; for in the Lord JEHOVAH is everlasting strength: Isaiah 26:3-4]

WHAT TO DO WHEN

PRAISE GOD AND WORSHIP HIM **WHAT TO DO WHEN –**
PRAISE GOD AND WORSHIP HIM – PRAISE GOD AND
WORSHIP HIM – PRAISE GOD AND WORSHIP HIM
The man you love marries someone else
PRAISE GOD AND WORSHIP HIM – PRAISE GOD AND
WORSHIP HIM – PRAISE GOD
God says NO!
WORSHIP GOD – WORSHIP GOD – WORSHIP GOD –
WORSHIP GOD – WORSHIP GOD
You want to get revenge
GOD BE PRAISED – GOD BE PRAISED – GOD BE PRAISED –
GOD BE PRAISED
Death comes unexpectedly
WORSHIP – WORSHIP – WORSHIP – WORSHIP – WORSHIP –
WORSHIP – WORSHIP
Friends hurt you
GLORIFY HIS NAME – GLORIFY HIS NAME – GLORIFY HIS
NAME – GLORIFY HIS NAME
When the enemy wants you to blame God
PRAISE – PRAISE – PRAISE – PRAISE – PRAISE – PRAISE –
PRAISE – PRAISE – PRAISE

God says wait
BLESS HIS NAME – BLESS HIS NAME – BLESS HIS NAME –
BLESS HIS NAME
Grief tries to attack you
PRAISE GOD AND WORSHIP HIM – PRAISE GOD AND
WORSHIP HIM – PRAISE GOD
The enemy comes in like a flood
GIVE HIM GLORY – GIVE HIM GLORY – GIVE HIM GLORY
– GIVE HIM GLORY
Hatred is trying to fill your heart
PRAISE – PRAISE – PRAISE – PRAISE – PRAISE – PRAISE –
PRAISE – PRAISE – PRAISE
You hear negative talk about you
WORSHIP GOD – WORSHIP GOD – WORSHIP GOD –
WORSHIP GOD – WORSHIP GOD
Loneliness comes
GOD BE PRAISED – GOD BE PRAISED – GOD BE PRAISED –
GOD BE PRAISED
You just don't know what to do
BLESS HIS NAME – BLESS HIS NAME – BLESS HIS NAME –
BLESS HIS NAME
Doubt concerning Gods promises occur
WORSHIP – WORSHIP – WORSHIP – WORSHIP – WORSHIP –
WORSHIP – WORSHIP – WORSHIP
Everything seems to be going wrong
GIVE HIM GLORY – GIVE HIM GLORY – GIVE HIM GLORY
– GIVE HIM GLORY
Confusion comes
PRAISE GOD AND WORSHIP HIM – PRAISE GOD AND
WORSHIP HIM
**At all times and for everything give thanks in the name of our
Lord Jesus Christ. Eph. 2:20**

The Visitation / Homegoing service

One night I had went to bed and was awakened by the sound of praise and worship; it was my pastor playing one of his tapes, preaching on the twentieth Psalms. It was around three thirty that morning:

> The Lord hear thee in the day of trouble, the name of the God of Jacob defend thee; Send thee help from the sanctuary and strength from out of Zion, remember all thy offerings and accept thy burnt sacrifice(Selah) Grant thee according to thine own heart. And fulfill all thy counsel. We will rejoice in thy salvation and in the name of our God. We will set up our banners: the Lord fulfill all thy petitions. Now know I that the Lord saveth his anointed; he will hear him from his holy heaven with the saving strength of his right hand, Some trust in chariots and some in horses, but we will remember the name of the Lord our God, they are brought down and fallen but we are risen and stand upright. Save Lord: let the King hear us when we call. Psalm 20 (KJV).

I can recall receiving a prophecy from my god daddy, Prophet F.B. I was married at the time; he said that the Lord said for me to grab a hold of these scriptures and keep them for the rest of my life, and I'm yet holding on to it. Anyway, I went up front where my Pastor was, along with D.L and Lena, they were lying on the floor, so I got on my knees at a chair, I listened to the sermon and began to praise God with tears streaming down my cheeks. I never once questioned God, because I knew in part, why he had taken my daughter and all other things that he wanted me to know will be revealed in his time. So upon returning back to bed, before getting in I heard this voice say to me, "get on your knees," in my mind I said, "I've just prayed," but I got on my knees anyway, with a puzzling look because I wondered why he wanted me on my knees again. So as soon as my right knee touched the floor I heard him say to me, "**I wanna be your best friend!** Whatever is bothering you, **Tell Me.** Who ever is bothering you, **Tell me.** Whatever you want me to do, **Tell Me.**" And his last words were, "**AND I WILL HANDLE IT!**" It was the Holy Spirit. So I began telling him about how the media had come out to the house questioning me and hopping on my daughter's weight saying she died of a heart attack, and how they were acting as if she was the only heavy child in the world. I said to him, "Will you please handle them for me, also, all of those children who picked on her at school, treated her nasty, funny, called her out her name making her life too hard for her to bear, will you take care of that for me please Holy Spirit, and help me and my family through this ordeal." And he handled it and is yet handling things, "Thank You Best Friend." I got up off my knees, got into bed listening to the gospel music that was playing on the TV satellite, when I say every song ministered to me, it really did. One particular morning as the music was playing, laying there after prayer with my eyes open, I know I wasn't sleep, when I saw this cloud appear before me and in the midst of the cloud God was holding Xenia by the left hand. At this point I wasn't paying attention to the music any more, I couldn't see her face for this fog like cloud, but I knew it was her, her body was slender and she was wearing pink. God said to me, "Do you Trust Me in this?" and I said, "Yes Lord," then he said, "well Xenia wanna know if you're gonna be alright?" and I said, "yes baby, I'm alright. He then allowed her to speak to me and she said, "I LOVE YOU MOMMY;" I began to cry and cry and cry saying back to her, "I LOVE YOU TOO BABY, WITH ALL MY HEART!" Soon as this was said and done, guess what song came on? Just because God said it, that's enough for me. He allowed my own song to minister to me. I cried even harder, but I knew then without a shadow of a doubt that her death was the perfect will of God, not just for her life, but for ours too.

Yea! My mother is coming! Was the phone call we had gotten, people were every where, flowers, cards, telegrams and all. But I was waiting for my Mama. Watching every car that pulled up, finally she arrived. Watching her get out of the car I started crying, I just needed to see her and now all I need is for her to hold me. Into the house she came looking for her fifth baby, how she managed to spoil all of us? I don't know. The moment we saw each other all she could say was, "Oh Shun, baby; only God knows, and we know that he doesn't make any mistakes." And from those words, she started praying. Standing right there as only she knows how to do. My mother is a POWRFUL! Woman of God. I heard some one call her, "a friend of God." If the devil is present, he won't be for long, because of the God in Mother Pace: the devil can't stand it. My mother is my number one role model and mentor; I wanted to be the same for my daughters. Later that night we received a phone call from one of my mother's friends in Philadelphia, Mom T. another Powerful Woman of God. I was awakened this time by the sound of prayer. She was praying with my Mother for the family, and for me. When I looked at my mother she signaled for me to pick up the other phone and I did, I heard Mom T. saying, "Mother all is well, I can only say what God give to me mother, and he said to tell you that all is well." I heard her say, "keep saying it mother until it gets into your spirit, and say it to Shun," then my mother said, "mom, she's on the phone," but mom T. was caught up in prayer and didn't hear her. So I said, "Mom, this is Shun, I hear you mom T," then she said to me, "Shun, the Lord said that all is well, and that he did this because you trust him. Now worship him!" I tried, but I was crying and saying, 'Thank You Jesus' real low and faint, then she said to me in a stern voice, "Open your mouth and worship him, babies can't worship in a time like this, but you've passed the baby stage. Open your mouth and worship your God." Honey let me tell you, I forgot about everything and every body, including Xenia and went for what I knew, and the God I know; and I opened my mouth and gave him all the glory. While I was worshiping God, this woman of God (Mom T.) said something to me that changed my life for ever. She said to me, "and we RELEASE her into the hands of a God who DID NOT make a mistake." Remember when I was in the hospital standing over Xenia, I had told her that I couldn't release her until God told me something, well he did, through Mom T. That's when I finally released her in my spirit; I knew it was God, because Mom T. was no where around when I spoke those words. Mom also said that God was going to reveal the all, in why he took Xenia. Little by little, my best friend (the Holy Spirit) is helping and teaching me how to deal with her absence from down here on earth. We can not fight against the will of God or the plan of God.

Before Mom T called, I couldn't eat or drink anything, but after I had a visit in His presence, I asked for something to eat. My mother started clapping her hands and praising God saying, "Thank You Jesus," and then she yelled up to the kitchen, "fix me something too." We all burst out laughing and could not stop, that was funny. I asked my mother how Phyllis was doing and did the operation go alright? She said that everything went well and that she was just resting, but no one had told her about Xenia. Some of the family was down there with her in Florida taking care of her, but when they got the news of Xenia's death; they needed some one to take care of them. They said each one of them would take turns going in to check on Phyllis. While one would go out to cry, the other one would stay with her, they did this for three days. While up here on the other end I told them we need to tell her, so I asked my best friend about it and he said to tell her on that Saturday. I said, "ya'll it's in my spirit to tell her now, after all she's all of the children's 'Auntie-mommy' and that's like not telling a mother her child is dead. So we called and they passed the phone to me. I was trying to sound all cheery and everything. I said, "hey girl, how are you?" and she said, "not good," I asked why, what's wrong, she said, " ya'll keeping something from me and I don't like it," then I chickened out and put the phone down, everybody asked what's wrong? I said she knows something, one sister said hang up the phone, I said, then she'll know for sure that something's wrong. I took a moment, picked the phone up again, but this time I said best friend, I need you to help me tell her. I said who's there with you? She said mother R. and some of the other saints, I said put mother R. on the phone please. I said mother, I'm getting ready to tell her about Xenia, so I need for you to hold her real tight and don't let her go. Then I asked her to put Phyllis back on the phone, I said, "Phyllis, the Lord saw fit to call Xenia home to be with him on Wednesday morning," I heard her groan, I felt the pain through the phone and she said, "Shun, Oh No! he did what?" she dropped the phone, mother R picked it up and I asked what was she doing. Mother said they had to lay her back on the bed and now she's crying. I said, "mother ya'll stay with her and to start praising God and worshipping him, and if they needed to call for the doctor, please do so; and let them know what's going on up here with the family.

I had heard so many different stories about what happened to Xenia at school. I was told she was eating and choked on food, I was told that she stood up at her desk, and told the teacher that she wasn't feeling well, but was ignored, then she fell to the floor. I was told that the nurse from across the way at the high school had to come and do CPR, because the nurse at the school where she attended didn't know it and when we went up to the school for answers, neither of the teachers were available, they made us wait in a room until the teacher left their classes. Which raised the question, why were they avoiding me? This man took us to her class room, I guess he was the assistant Principal, I don't know. When we got into her class room, I asked where my daughter's desk was, and he pointed to a desk in the back of the class all by it self, away from the other students. Teachers can be something else too, when they want to be. I asked why she was separated from the others. He just shrugged his shoulder in an 'I don't know' motion. None of my questions were answered. But I know that my best friend is going to handle it. The truth shall be revealed. We received an anonymous phone call, saying we need to sue the school for negligence, the person did not leave a name, but they knew a close friend who worked there, who knew what happened. Then a close friend of the family came over to see me saying the same things. Only this time it was from some of the students that went to the school, and being a mother, I began to get upset. My feelings were beginning to turn bad, and then the Holy Spirit said to me, "I told you not to get caught up with the preliminaries, I told you before she hit the ground, I took her". The cost of the funeral was well over eighteen thousand dollars; long story short, my church (Holy Trinity C.O.G.I.C.), the pastors in the city, and donations that were sent in the sympathy cards paid for everything. At first my love said that he was going to pay half, and then he changed it and said that he would only pay his half if he saw my half of the money first. And he had insurance on both girls, so the Lord blessed me with my half, then the owner of the funeral home called us and said that your love has refused to pay his half and that they need their monies. So there I was stuck with the bill, but God came through for me. (Call to me and I will answer you and show you great and mighty things...Jer. 33:3a)

Bishop E. P. Upon our request, allowed us to use his facilities at no charge. God bless you Bishop, and your church. The church holds about ten thousand people and there were about six thousand or more a Xenia's home going service on a Monday evening at 2:00 p.m. February the twenty six in the year of our Lord two thousand one. When we were getting ready to come into the church (for some reason his family didn't want to wait, so they were already seated) I had my head down, trying to be the mourning mother, but before I could enter the church my best friend said to me, "why is your head down? Lift up your head." I picked my head up and began to speak to the people standing as we were coming in, saying hello, how are you, hey I'm so glad to see you, hi, God bless you. I was saying Thank you Holy Ghost! Lord hold me, be with me best friend, I was just worshipping God. When I got to the casket, yes I cried and gave her a kiss, then went to my seat. But not for long, because the Holy Spirit said, "get to the microphone and sing! I took off and M.E. was running behind me saying, "Shun where are you going, you alright?" I said, "I've got to get to the microphone. The family was yet coming in, when I began to sing, something happened to me. I felt strength like never before. My mother told me later that when she heard my voice, she said, "Lord, if she can praise you and this is her child, then surely I can praise him too," and she began to dance in the spirit. Soon the people were dancing and praising God all over the sanctuary. It wasn't a funeral at all; it was more like a church service. My mother wanted to have a wake at their church (Rehoboth Deliverance Center C.O.G.I.C. in Barnesville, Georgia about forty five to fifty minutes south of Atlanta, we had church there too, they even rolled the casket to the side and had an alter call. This was and is my prayer; that God would use her death to bring young people to him.

Mean while, back to the service. Mr. C. called my sisters up to sing with him, "It won't hurt any more" they were crying and holding each other up, but those girls sang! Her school chorus did her favorite song by M. M. "Take the shackles off my feet so I can dance," and for the first time I heard the lyrics to the song, I began to cry harder saying to myself, "Lord my child was trying to tell me something." She performed this song in the talent show at Campbell Elementary School, and again at her middle school. I had to buy that CD twice for her, because she broke the first one by mistake. Her favorite movie was "Save the last dance."

My god daddy had to leave the service early because he had to preach that night, so he came over to where we (my friend and I) were standing at the time, and he said to my friend, "young man you are right for her and the Lord said don't go no where." When he said those words, I was puzzled and I said to myself, "why would God say to him, don't go no where?" Now I know why, because I was going with him and he was going some where else, to marry somebody else four days later. Now I understand why God tells us things in part, because if he showed us everything, we would hurt some folk and they would hurt us; and we'd all be dead or in jail. Thank you Lord for hiding me from the all and only letting me know when I'm able to handle it.

Our final goodbye

S itting here under the same green tent I would see so many times
as I traveled passing different cemeteries, not knowing that one
day I would be sitting under one of them. Starring at the casket
saying this is it, after they do the ashes to ashes and dust to dust I'd
have to leave my baby for good. But before we left, we released a
bunch of balloons, pink, blue, and white, it was a beautiful sight to
see all the balloons flying away, which made me cry because I
thought of the Flight that she took on February 21, 2001. Two
weeks later; I was going to visit the grave sight, and in my mind I
was saying, I'm going to cry and cry, and cry; I'm going to have a
crying (pity) party, I'm going to talk to her and get my cry on; so I
got there, walked over to where the fresh dirt and straw was, and
my best friend said to me, now you can cry if you want too, I won't
stop you, But she's not down there, she's with me. At that moment I
looked up towards heaven and began to smile, and then I started
laughing; I said, "girl, I'll see you later" I walked to my car; got in,
and went home. I've only been to her grave sight twice, once for her
Birthday August 31, she would have been twelve, and the second
time was when P. Magazine did an interview about her and we took
pictures, other than that, I have no intentions of going back. Now
it's just me and Aarion; not that we couldn't stay where we were,
but I saw no need to stay in a two bedroom, when they slept with

me anyway, and now that Xenia was gone, I moved into a one bedroom apartment up the street, brand new. My sister Duranice told me latter that she was taking the children for a ride one day, and they road to the very complex we moved into, just riding around and Xenia made a statement about how nice it would be if we lived there because they were nicer than where we were. Anyway sitting at the table in the new place; getting ready to eat our first dinner, there we were preparing to say grace, when I reached out my one hand to Aarion and the other one automatically went to where Xenia would have been sitting, and I opened my mouth to say grace and couldn't, (I started crying) because I noticed that I had reached out to her and she wasn't there. And Aarion got up out of her seat, drew closer to me, she started rubbing my back; and said to me, go ahead and cry Mama; because there's healing in your tears. (Psalms 126: 5) They that sow in tears shall reap in joy.

The Reading of
Xenia's Head Stone

Xenia Pace Rhodes

Sunrise   Sunset
8-31-89   2-21-01

Eleven years of heaven on earth

And we release you into the hands of a God
who did not make a mistake

CHAPTER THREE

My Daily Diary

<u>Unclothe</u>

But Lord, He Married Someone Else

It was March 2,2001 when he married, which I didn't find out until the day after Memorials Day, what a poignant experience,(well kill me, why don't cha). I had just buried my daughter February 26, 2001. So, you may say apart of me was already dead. He came down to Atlanta to be with me for the home going service, holding my hands, comforting me, crying with me...(now I wonder if the tears were for me, my daughter or what he was about to do four days later). God! He married somebody else. Let's go back to how we met: two years after I had given birth to my second daughter (Aarion) and three years after my divorce. Gospel plays were really taking off, but I wasn't interested, I had done a few but because they didn't want to pay me my price or I had done the show and they didn't want to pay me because they did not make the money at the box office, so they would tell me. So I stopped plays altogether. But one day after 12:00 noonday service, one of the college students came up to me and said, "sister Shun can I tell you what the Lord told me to tell you," I said, "yes," he said, "you've been turning down plays" (my mouth was open and my eyes bucked), but the Lord said, "plays are going to be one of the main vehicles that he's going to use to bring souls to him and you are to be apart of this move, so the next play that comes along, take it. Besides the word, a minister at my church, Elder M. C. came to me and said, "God had strategically designed and orchestrated for me to meet my husband to be." And then I said, "oh no not another word," yes another word from the Lord saying how he would look, a full description.

Well a call came in for a play entitled, "A fool and His money" paying at the time what I thought was good money. I'm divorced with two beautiful .daughters (2 and 6). The only thing on my mind was taking care of us three: me, myself and mine. No men in sight or on my mind, well not totally, there was a thought or two on the old ex in Texas. (Smile) I tell every one that I was going with him, because he definitely wasn't going with me. (Laugh) Anyway, I'd be making ex amount of dollars a Sunday, for the next six months, O boy, I could get a house and everything else we wanted or needed. But little did I know I was going to meet Mr. Player. The rehearsals were in Dallas, TX. Where my ex boyfriend lived, but Mr. Player was the acting coach for us who knew nothing, he knew it all; so I started trusting him. Then we started talking about our children, he had two and so did I. So the beginning of a friendship had begun. After about two weeks of rehearsals we broke for Thanksgiving. We returned to Dallas for two more weeks of rehearsals, while getting our luggage, he asked me and my sister (Latrice), did we miss him during the break? Latrice said, "No!" But me feeling bad at my sister's cold response said yes we did, my sister looked like, speak for yourself, then I said, well I missed you. I'm just too soft hearted, loving, kind, gullible, taking people at face value and their word. Like I said, my Texas ex was there, I would call him to see how he was doing. We went to church a few times, I visited his job, he set a date with me, but only me went (he was a no show and a no call). We were to go to a Seafood place to eat and then go to the movies. Well I waited for him to pick me up, he never came. So I called his house, he wasn't there. I called his job, they said he had left over an hour ago. Then I called back to his house to leave a message, letting him know that I was going to take a taxi to the restaurant and wait for him, that if we missed each other there, then I'd meet him at the movies. I ate and saw the movie by myself. He never called to say what happened, but he did call to ask me if I would go to church with him that Sunday, and I said No! But you can explain why you stood me up. To be honest I don't know what he said, all I know is I was through. Plus there were times we would go out; I would ride with him to a venue. Then upon time to leave he would ask me to ride back with my aces (Tarsha and Kristie), because he had to take his god son home or he had to go to work. I even invited him to one of the rehearsals to see me work, he said he'd come, but he was a no show. And all the while Mr. Player saw what was going on. Once I had an engagement while in Texas and they sent a limousine to pick me up. Now instead of me riding in my ride, I got in my ex in Tex car to ride with him and while we were together I asked him what was going on with us, where were we headed. Now the ride to the church was about a thirty to forty minute ride and he said nothing all the way there. I even asked if he heard my question and he said yea, but still no answer. So I left him alone, cause we were going nowhere slow. Well we broke again until after Christmas, returning the beginning of the year to start the play (January through June. The longest I've been away from my girls or home, well from the first opening night in Dallas, until he left the show at the beginning of April. He would come back stage to kiss me (on the cheek) and tell me to have a good show. Every single night he did this. And if someone was in the audience that night, he wanted me to empress, he would tell me to wear it out, do this or try that the next time I was on stage. All of which would make the audience go wild. This made me trust him even more, because the acting tips and things he said to do worked.

One night he came back stage to do his little regular routine of kisses and some times hugs, telling me to have a good show, but I was no where to be found. I hid behind the stage just to see what he would do. I heard him asking every body, 'have ya'll seen Shun'. He was running all over the place looking for me. It went from just looking for me, to really looking for me, because I opened up the show. I heard him run up the steps to where I was supposed to be, not there. Boy, did I have fun. Besides, more than one person had told me that he liked me, so I had to see. One guy who was with the show told me of the barriers that a guy would try to keep, trying not to let a girl know that he liked her. Well his were down and the other guys with the show knew it, my sister and her friend; who said to

me he has the hots for you girl and he's in love with you. I asked her
how did she know, her response was, he told me. Not only did he
come back stage every night to kiss me and tell me to have a good
show. One of those times after kissing me, he said, "I love you".
And after we started traveling on the road with the show, he would
come to our room every night, stay for a while and leave. I thought
nothing of it because a few of the cast members would come by at
times to talk or just hang out and then leave. So I thought this was
what he was doing, but my sister knew better. She would ask me,
"Why is he coming here all the time, every night." I said, "I don't
know! Ask him". I knew when it was him at the door, because when
my sister went to the door to answer the knock she would give this
great big sigh, not caring if he heard her or not, saying, "God! Him
again, what does he want?" Trying to be a good Christian, she
would open the door, not saying hello, walking away as he came in.
He went from coming and leaving to coming and staying the night,
sleeping on the floor at the foot of my bed. In spite of my sister
Latrice not wanting him around, he came any way. Honest to God, I
thought nothing of what he was doing or trying to do. My thoughts
were all spiritual; he wasn't saved, so I thought he just enjoyed our
company like everyone else. We are good folk to be around, if we
like you or not. (Smile)

We would call home all the time, so one day during a phone call
home, I was talking to my oldest sister (Duranice), telling her what
was going on and she said, "the Lord wanted us to minister to him
and that he needed help from God." Also speaking with our mother,
she encouraged us to let the love of God shine through us; living
holy and don't get caught up in a bunch of mess out there on the
road, stay prayful; all of which we did. So after that phone conversation, witnessing to him was my only focus. By this time we were
in Kansas City, he's in my dressing room all the time, so I started
witnessing to him about Jesus and how he needed to give his life to
the Lord. He told me about his children's mother, that they were not
together and that he was dealing with a whole lot of drama. So I
again said, "you need to get save and marry that girl, she loves
you.:" I didn't know her, but I put myself in her shoes and if that
was me I would definitely want the guy to marry me, was what I

said to him. But he just sat there on the wall to wall counter starring at me while I was putting on my makeup, getting ready for the show that night. Not only was he good looking, but he fitted the description of the prophecy I had gotten, the only thing—he wasn't saved. We started being around each other a lot, going to breakfast some mornings, not by ourselves but with some of the other cast members. He heard me mention that I liked shrimp, so he shows up at my door. While looking through the peep hole, one hand was behind his back. I opened the door and he handed me a plate of shrimp, he had ordered from room service. My album "A Wealthy Place" had just hit the market while with the show, and he would buy me a bill board magazine to keep up with where I was on the charts. He would help me with my bags and everybody knows the guys that travel with shows, they help no one, but them selves. He was different, if he saw me with my bags, he would offer to help. And every lady loves a gentleman. But he was not saved, and I knew this, but in the back of my mind was 'but God can save him' and he can, he will save anybody who wants to be saved. Anyway my feelings started changing from us just being friends to more than a friend. I heard that if you spend time with anyone long enough you could grow to like them, now that's the truth. We were with each other everyday for three months, not in your face together, but around each other. I knew where he was most of the time and one of those most places were "the strip clubs" he loved himself some women, I think that's what turned me on to him, a real man. I would get on him from time to time about going, but all he'd say was, pray for me gospel Pace, or Ms. Pace. Heineken was his drink, anyway I accepted him for who he was and what he was. He knew where I was all the time, because after the show every night, I would change and head straight for the hotel, I didn't hang out, nor did I go to any of the cast parties, in my room was safety. I did go to eat every now and then with the cast, it was one of those times where he found out that I had been married technically for nine and a half years, and never experienced an Or——. I didn't find out my self until one day my girlfriend was over to my house after Sunday service and we were talking girl talk, when we got on the subject about the "O" word, so I asked her what was it? She said

"Shun!" you don't know what an Or—— is? She then went on to tell me what happens when you've experienced it, and I said, I have never felt anything like that or even close to it, she fell in the floor laughing, then she said I'm sorry, but girl you've been married for how long? And now you're pregnant with your second child and you haven't experienced the highest peak of love making? I said "Nope," she couldn't believe it and I couldn't believe that I had missed out on this feeling that was to take me to heaven and back. She said girl you're the first I've seen, you're still a virgin she said, pregnant and all, so that's how I found out.

I don't know (at the table with the cast) how the subject came up, but it did. I was at one end of the table with my sister and the ladies and the guys were at the other end, when I heard Mr. player say "man she was moving like a fish out of water," I was looking down in that direction, then he said, you know what I'm talking bout gospel Pace? And everybody looked at me, (child I was so green, that if I was on grass, you couldn't have seen me) I was so embarrassed, I couldn't say a word, then one of the guys said hey, don't be shame, I know plenty of women like that, in church and out, it aint yo fault, I blame the guy. I was so glad to leave and get back to the room, but I guess that gave player something to work towards, men love to conquer.

Anyway like I said we were friends first, I would buy his children things and he would buy my girls things, I even bought him a bible with his name on it, I found out later that I spelled his name wrong, so I bought him another one, this time I spelled it right, I went to his room to give it to him, he had just gotten up and was brushing his teeth , I didn't stay long, but upon leaving, walking down the hall,(he was watching me) I turned around, he said, "thank you," and I said, "you're welcome," and continued to walk. Then I remembered him saying that night that he loved me, so I turned around again and said, "do you remember telling me the other night back stage that you loved me?" he said, "yes". Then I asked him, "were you serious?" he said, "of course," then I told him, "Now I know what the S in your name stands for. He said, "Oh No! Not you gospel pace," I said, "I didn't say the word, I just said the letter," and we both laughed. There were some cities we had to fly into and he would get his seat next to mine if he could. Or he would swap seats with a cast member that was sitting next to me; he'd hold my hand for take off. We would listen to music together for a little while, then he had to read his paper, my mind went to when I was a little girl, how I loved to see my daddy read the news paper. I don't know what about it that turns me on, but it does. So when I saw him reading his paper I was taken and not just reading the paper, but all of the little nice things he'd done. I was falling in love slowly but surely. I said, "Lord, I'm in love with a sinner." So knowing this I began to pray, saying, "Now Lord, this man fits the prophecy you gave to me and I love him; if he's my husband then I need you to save him." Easter was coming up within a few weeks, so I said, "Lord if he's for me save him on Easter Sunday, like you filled my daddy with the Holy Ghost on a Easter. Long story short, he got save, but he wouldn't tell me and one of the guys with the show, who was saved too, saw what I saw. He came to me and asked, "does Player look different to you?" and I said, "yes he does," then he said, "He's saved, I know that look, he looks lighter," and I began to laugh, I was a happy sister. I approached him asking later, had he gotten saved, he started laughing and said, "Yea." Once he had to leave the show, but was coming back. When he left we were in one city and when he returned we would be in Connecticut. Any way it was opening night, we had got to the theatre early as usual, sitting in my dressing room putting on my makeup, I heard his voice and my heart leaped. I put my hand to my chest leaning forward and said, "Oh my God! It's him, he's here." Latrice said, "Who?" I called his name and said he's here. She went to the door, opened it looking up and down the hall, then she said, "I don't see nobody," I said, "I don't care, he's here." And sure enough he came to my door, knocked and I said, "Who is it?" and he did the famous 'YO' and came in. I was smiling so big, I wanted to hug him, but I wanted him to reach out first. So I began to sit back down when he said, "Yo, what's up, you can't hug a brother?" Then we hugged with him squeezing my chest, he always gave such nice hugs and smelled so good; around his neck was a place I could stay forever. It was there in Connecticut where I met his children and their mother. He came to me during the Saturday matinee and said that they would be coming to the night show, and that she had found a note-book of his and inside was some love cards that I had given him. Then I asked, "So, she know about me?" he shrugged his shoulder like, 'I don't know'. After the show I started getting upset, my feelings were confused; did he love me, or what? So confiding with a guy in the show, he asked, is he bringing her, or is she coming. I said, "Coming", then he said, "well, you have nothing to worry about." On the other hand, if he was bringing her, then I would tell you to leave him alone. Any way they came, he brought one of his children back to my dressing room, introduced us and said this is the lady who has been giving you all those toys. Then after the show is when I met the other child and their mother. She looked me up and down, checking me out. The van was getting ready to leave and I had to go. Then he handed me his things to take back in front of her, which made me think that this was his way of telling her I was the new woman in his life now. Well the time for him to leave the show was coming, as well as his Birthday. He was leaving a week before it would come, so I was planning how I could celebrate his birthday before he left. So that night at the show before he was to leave the next day, we were sitting down stage on the floor. The pit was lowered, so sitting there I asked him what he wanted for his birthday? He said, "a lap dance," I said, "how do you do that?" He laughed and said never mind. So the morning he was to leave, I took him down stairs to breakfast. Then we sat in the hotel lounge and talked for a while. Then we went back to his room, I helped him finish packing and then we laid on the bed hugged up together talking about us. I had to make him kiss me; he said he wasn't a kisser. I should have known then, that he wasn't for me. Any way we were leaving as well, going to the next city, I was so sad. I didn't want him to leave, but we both had to go. I was going to kiss him but he didn't want anybody to see us. After he left, he stayed in touch calling every now and then. It's June and the show was coming to an end. He came out one last time before the show ended, we got each others information. He flew back home and I came back to Atlanta, home with my girls and family again. I told my girls about the man I'd met and from me telling them how he was, them seeing me happy, he had their approval way before they met him.

We had moved into a new place of our own and I had a new man. He would call and talk to me and my girls. One day I asked him if he would be my manager, I trusted him number one, and second I loved him which was enough for me. So here we are back together again every weekend and sometimes through the week, depending on the engagements, if it was a conference or a concert. Now it was just me and him, sometimes the promoters would send for me, the singers and the band. But for the most part it was just me and my manager. We went across the country together and even over seas, we had a good time. But it was dajavu, a different kind, but still dajavu. The only thing was; I was married to the first one and this one I wasn't. The first one liked roosters, the second one liked chicks. It's been three years now and I had been doing good, loving the Lord and trying to live saved. I almost slipped one time in New York; I jumped up and ran into the bathroom. It started by him putting on some music, asking me to dance for him. I found out what a lap dance was. While in the bathroom, looking in the mirror, I began to cry. I couldn't believe I had done what I just did. I was hurt, I thought about my mother, way in New York, my mother was on my mind and that God was going to show her or tell her; so that made me scared. Then I thought about God. I was scared of my mother before I was scared of God, and that's the truth. I didn't like hurting no body, but to hurt my mother was devastating! Anyway, I was dancing and he came up behind me, started touching me and kissing me on my neck. I had NEVER been touched like that before. The next thing I knew, I was on my back on the bed and his hands were where they wasn't suppose to be and that's as far as it went, that time. He said that he was sorry and that he had no business doing that. I said, "no, its was my fault, I didn't know me dancing was going to do that." When I was married and not being satisfied, I asked my husband what was it I could do to make our love making better? He said, "Nothing." But now here I am with a man who says anything goes. He wanted to please me, but he was not my husband, which brought me to the point of jumping up. Because it was **WRONG!** But playing with fire, you will get burned. It took a while, but it happened. We were on a concert date on the North West coast. I thought I was having a heart attack, once again I jumped up and sat on the floor, he said do you want me to sit with you? I said no, then standing at the window crying, thinking okay, what's wrong with you? Then I stopped all together, he would wonder why I was acting the way I was. I told him that it's wrong and I can't do that any more. Well this went on and off for four years, even up to after the death of my baby and he was married, but I didn't know it. The devil had made a fool out of me, and was laughing in my face. This is why I say in my testimony that after the death of my daughter, I just got saved, 2001. Yes, traveling, singing, preaching and telling God, I'm sorry, but never **REPENTING!** The very thing I despised and said I'd never do, I was doing it: sleeping with a man I wasn't married to. Whatever it takes for God to bring you to him or back to him, **HE'S GOING TO DO IT**. Now if you rebuff his warnings then woe to you. [The crown is fallen from our head: woe unto us that we have sinned! Lam. 5: 16.] Yes there was a time in my life when I was really going after God and I loved him. But I had no relationship with him and the place where he wanted me, I wasn't there. So, therefore the work I was suppose to do, I could not do [This I say then, Walk in the Spirit, and ye shall not fulfill the lust of the flesh. For the flesh lusteth against the Spirit and the Spirit against the flesh and these are contrary the one to the other; so that ye cannot do the things that ye would. Gal. 5:16-17]. Fasting sometimes and then waiting three months or better, mostly better, then fasting again, the same with reading my Bible. I would read It sometimes and then it would be months before I even looked at it. Talking about a solid foundation, let's just say I had no foundation. So when the devil and his demons came they knew that I had NOTHING. So I was putty in the devil's hands, I had opened myself up to be possessed by demon spirits, witchcraft, curses and endangering the life of my girls spiritually and naturally, because I was the head of my household and what happens to the head, trickles down through the family.

Dates, Times & Places

MAY 28, 2001

We are at my sister's house, having a good time when someone asked me about Mr. Player and how he was doing? I said that I hadn't heard from him in awhile and I didn't know what was going on. Then I said, "If it's over then so be it, but it seems like he could be man enough to tell me at least," and Latrice said, "Good! Move on." So, I asked her if she had heard from him. Because she had grew to love him and he would talk to her at times by cell phone, but she said no. My sisters are good to me, they knew then; but no one said a word. They laughed and played music, watched movies and I played my favorite game 'Scrabble' yea. I can hear some people in Detroit now, yea. Detroit put your money where your mouth is. (Smile) it's me, you, god mommy P. and who ever else you want to play, it's on. Come on, all you other players, if you think you can beat me, then bring it, cause I have already broughten it, (smile, joke).

May – 01

The school gave a special service in honor of the students and teachers who had pass that year. After the gathering, my mother came up to me saying, " I need to speak with you later on today if I can," she went on to say, "you know that sometimes in life the things that happens to us is not always to hurt us, but it's for our good," I said, "yes ma'am, I know." Then she said, "well remember that when I talk to you," I said, "yes ma'am mother." But all while she's talking, I'm saying in my head, what's up? What is she going to talk to me about? The day before that, my Pastor was on the phone and he said that he needed to talk to me about something, then her come Latrice my sister saying she needed to talk to me. I said, "Okay now, this is the third, I need to talk to yous; now what's going on?" So when my mother, my pastor and my sister, made it known that they needed to talk to me, then my spiritual antennas went up. I started checking myself out, had I said something wrong to somebody or did something. Why does everybody need to talk to me? Boy, did I find out.

June 2, 01

Questions were filling my head, is she pregnant? Was he sleeping with the both of us, at the same time? Did he ever really love me? Or was I a 'in the mean time fling'? Did he love me at all? Why was he in my life for four years? Having me on hold. I remember back in June, he was doing his play in a south east state and the both of us were there, she and I. But, I thought I had nothing to worry about, because he made me feel so secure in us, me and him. I knew he loved her, but it was only because she was his children's mom, that was what he told me and I believed him. Love will make you blind and stupid.

I feel sick to my stomach! I feel used, betrayed, cut off; my heart is bleeding so profusely, none stop. Holy Spirit, best friend please hold my heart, I can't feel it any more. I'm going on about my daily things, but truly I'm being carried or more like dragged along. Not wanting to go but I must keep going. What's next? I'm not looking for another love, how can I when he has my heart and is in my spirit. Because when you sleep with someone you both partake of each other's spirit, that's why God only meant for sex or love making to be between a husband and a wife. Please know that writing these things and sharing my life with you doesn't make me feel good or proud, but God has a woe behind me. He told me to tell it and hold nothing back. I told him, "Lord if this is going to help some woman or man, then I'll tell it, my shame for his glory". If you, right now call yourself save, and you're sleeping around; you are not! **REPENT!** And ask the Lord to forgive you and cleanse you and sever every spirit that may have come into your spirit, and wash you in the blood of Jesus Christ. Now live Holy and wait on God to bring the mate he wants you to have in your life. I asked myself more questions, what if he comes back. Can I accept him, the children along with her? Because they will forever be apart of his life. Yes, I can? Or Yes, I can't, this means apart of you say yes and another part says no. Do you just want him just so you can say, I got him and she didn't? Just what would be the real reason you would want him back? And I answered myself truthfully, which was; because I had loved him so UNCODITIONALLY, I would be willing to take him back, nothing more, and nothing less. Yes, I know that God can give me someone else, and we'd be happy together, but a small part of my heart will always belong to him, just like I know part of my heart is in his heart and to me that's just like being unfaithful, because all of you isn't there; you're with one person, but your mind is with another person. There are a lot of men you can love, but then there is that one man who has it all. You're not just friends, but you're soul mates, that are the man you need to marry. There were some good things I learned and one of the things I learned most was how to love people for whom and what they are. I feel like I can never love again, but God allows these experiences to happen to let us know that He wants nothing and no one else to be first in our lives except Him. [Thou shalt have none other gods before me. Deut. 5:7].

June 4, 10

Today I'm trying to read the word of God, but thoughts of what's happened keep coming to my head. When I woke up this morning, me eyes were sooooo heavy as well as my spirit. Oh, Holy Spirit, best friend, oh that you would lift this load, the shame I feel, because I thought I had a boyfriend, fiancé, a husband to be. Oh the hurt and embarrassment seems like the world knows. He called and left me a message June first, saying we needed to talk, and what he had done was out of the blue (what does this phrase really mean?) Please! I don't want to start hating the color blue, this was my daughter's favorite color, and blue had nothing to do with it. What about 'U'. Anyway, he said he really felt bad about the whole thing and that he was dealing with so much stuff, so that's why we need to talk. He wants to tell me how it happened, what went down and all of the particulars, then he said that he really, really, truly loved me and that I was his sweetheart and will always be his sweetheart.

June 5, 01

Today I feel sick, hopeless, lost, just on a real low, disastrous, yuck. Why do I feel this way? The man of my heart, married someone else: Why? Witchcraft; Lord, I pray that your Spirit, the Holy Ghost himself lift me from this deep pit of lost love I feel like I'm in. When I got the news on the 29, after Memorials Day, my sister Latrice called, asking if she could come over, I said sure. She, Melonda, and Duranice came over, they were sitting in the living room with me and Latrice said, "Shun I'm not one hundred percent sure, but I am ninety percent sure," I said, "okay." Then she said, "Player is married, and it happened March 2, 01. All I could say was Okay; she was crying, and I was numb. Have you ever been so hurt you couldn't feel it? For a few moments I was just there, Latrice said, "girl you are so strong," I said, "girl, God has taken me out of myself and all I see is how strong he has made me," then tears began to roll down my face, they asked if I was going to be alright? I said, "Yea, I'll be fine, I just need to be alone," they cleared out, but assured me of their support. When they left, I just walked around in my apartment, thinking and wondering, trying to remain rational. To myself I was saying, "So that explain the abrupt, all of a sudden no more phone calls, no nothing! Feels like another death has happened to me, first I lost my daughter, February 21, and buried her on the 26, with him right by my side holding my hands, comforting me, knowing all the time that he was going to get married to his children's mom; now this is what I call, B.M.D". So I returned his call as he requested, I had to leave a message because he did not answer. I wonder why? Anyway, I told him that I yet cared for him, and loved him and that I would be waiting for him to call me back.

It's been three days now, and I haven't heard from him yet. If I could only stop crying, if only the hurt could go away and this aching in my head would leave. This thing that's resting on my chest, if it would just lift, I'm trying to take deep breaths, but they won't come. "But I've got the Victory;" well it showll don't feel like it! Why is it that when bad news come everybody knows before you do?

June 8, 01

Just getting back from a concert date in Kansas, but while I was there he called me again on my cell phone. This was the third time he had called, so I changed my number. I had asked him to call my house, because I knew that the conversation was going to be long and I didn't want a high cell phone bill. Besides, when we were going together, well, when I was going with him, for the most part I did all the calling, yes he did call but when he did he made sure that he didn't talk long, he always had to go some where, well at least that's what he would tell me.

How do I deal with the sadness I feel? The loneliness? I feel like apart of my heart has been ripped out. On the plane coming home all I could do was cry and talk to the Holy Spirit, my best friend and ask him how could someone who say that they love you so much, hurt you so bad? One morning in my prayer time, I asked my best friend a question, mind you this was way before I knew anything; I asked him what was going on with Mr. Player? And why haven't I heard from him in almost a month and some weeks? He then said to me and I quote, "he's operating under the spirit of witchcraft," and that was all he told me. Now, I asked him why you couldn't have told me back then that he was married. He said to me, "Because you could not have handled it." I didn't ask any more questions.

Witchcraft is something else; the person who it's being worked on doesn't even have a clue about what's going on. And they don't know that they're being controlled by an unseen demonic spirit, they will do things and don't know why: But unless the Spirit of the Lord reveal it and that yoke be destroyed they will forever be bound.

I had lunch with my sisters today and shared some things with them of how I was feeling, I told them that I would be turning forty this year and that I just don't feel like I can put forth the energy, time, effort nor love into another relationship, and that I felt like I would be better off with just me and my daughter. I told them that at times, I can hardly breathe; but I know that life goes on. I shared that I felt like second best, there is no second best if it's not first, then it's nothing but next, this is how I'd feel, if I went back, but one of my sisters interrupted me and said, "No, she's next, because he's in love with you and his heart is with you," is that right, I said, well all I know is that, I don't want to talk to anybody else. I don't want to get to know anybody else, it's just too hurting; all the acts of kindness you give, your heart and soul, spirit, mind, as well as your emotions, giving your money and giving your honey. I don't know if I feel sorry for him or for me. Thinking that he's going to marry you, so you just get stupid and don't think, that's the real deal; all I know is, I'm just trying to take this blow one day at a time, just like the death of my daughter: I still have my moments.

I remember the day after receiving the news that he had gotten married. After dropping my daughter Aarion off at school. Soon as I got back to the house I fell on the ottoman screaming and hollering, "God you got to help me, I can't take this pain." He then whispered gently to me, "Praise me right there, in the midst of the pain you are feeling, praise me. And thank me for him marring somebody else."

Yes, I love God, Jesus and the Holy Spirit and I ain't going no where. In fact I told him one day while riding up the street in my little mini van, hurting and crying; I told God, "I didn't leave you while going through a divorce and carrying a baby at the same time, I didn't leave you when after the divorce and times got hard, couldn't buy a bar of soap, all we had was a can of Lysol spray cleaning our bodies the best way we could, I didn't leave you when you decided to take my first born, and only you know that, that was the hardest thing I've ever had to go through, so I shoal ain't gonna let no Nigga, now make me turn my back on you. Because you've been too good to me!!! Then I told God, his hair ain't curly enough, his skin ain't light enough and his stuff ain't big enough for me to stop loving God and loose my soul. Yea, sin is pleasurable, but the end result of sin is death. And sometimes it's a spiritual death and sometimes it's a natural death, and then it could be both. But every man is tempted, when he is drawn away of his own lust and enticed. Then when lust hath conceived, it bringeth forth sin; and sin, when it is finished, bringeth forth death.

I've prayed, I've danced, I've shouted, I've screamed, I've exhaled, I've inhaled and I'm in hell. He still won't leave my mind. If I could get him off my mind, and out of my heart, I think I would be alright. I say, think because, if I totally forget about him, will it mean that I never really loved him or what? See women, how following after the flesh can have you messed up and even you men too. This I say then, Walk in the Spirit, and ye shall not fulfil the lust of the flesh. For the flesh lusteth against the Spirit, and the Spirit against the flesh: and these are contrary the one to the other: so that ye cannot do the things that ye would. (Gal. 5:16 & 17). Why didn't I see this coming? He just left me high and dry, I was in the midst of my recording session without a manager, yes, he was my manager too, dejavue, yes only this one I wasn't married to. How could he?

I've just tried to call his cell again, but the guy at the other end said that I had a wrong number, was it a wrong number? Or was he avoiding me? Or did he change his number because I changed mine? Whatever, I feel sick to my stomach again, I want to cry but I can't, should I call back to make sure or just leave it alone? But what do I do with the questions I have that needs answering? I'm trying to study and prepare for a sermon, I have to preach in Rockingham, N.C. tomorrow, and Lord I really desperately need your help,

HELP!

June 14, 01

I did my last attempt to try and reach him. Let me just face the truth; he has done me lower than any man on the face of this earth, along with my love. What he did was dirty and low down, why couldn't he tell me? All I know is, I need to keep writing; each day it helps me to deal with the hurt, the pain, the feeling of being dumped, the feelings of rejection, that cut off feeling, thrown to the side, well more like slung. I had a dream about him, it was a powerful dream. Let's just say, I'm glad it was only a dream.

Then I woke up, knowing that it was a dream gave me a big relief, Thank You Jesus!

Well, I'm in Rockingham, N. C. I have to go and preach with a broken heart, I asked my best friend, the Holy Ghost to please help me! And he did, something strange happened to me tonight while I was preaching, I shared with the congregation my testimony, the hurt I was going through, telling them in spite of, whatever may be going on in their lives, we are to yet Praise God! When all of a sudden my head started spinning around, I thought I was going to fall but I held on to the podium until it stopped. The same thing happened to me when I was on the phone talking to his mother concerning him getting married and was it true, my sister and my god mother told me that it was an attack sent from the devil, but it won't work; you're covered in the Blood of Jesus. Several women came up to me tonight saying, how much they were touched by my testimony: all praises go to God, He's carrying me. I'm leaving here tomorrow going to Greensboro, N.C. if the lords will.

It's a new day, I woke up this morning with a very bad headache, maybe I ate too late before going to bed, or maybe he's just that heavy on my mind. I know you may be saying girl, it's been three months, going on four, but I didn't find out until the day after memorials day, however it doesn't matter how long, the pain says, it just happened; the question I asked myself this morning was, Shun take away how you felt when he touched you as a man, you have never had a real intercourse experience with him, every thing was always quick and satisfying him (dajavue). Once or twice I was really pleased, but it wasn't with his genital organ, it was hands only. Take all of this away and remember some of the conversations ya'll have had, and think about the kind of person he really is, think about the times when he didn't make you feel like a lady, he was trying at times but it's really not down on the inside of him, some things was a front. He said to me in a conversation once, that he would have a hard time dealing, if he had to go back to a nine to five, because his love was theatre and movie production, I thought about, now if I marry him what would I be doing until his big break came? Holding down the fort (dejavue), again, he even told me that he'd never do anything to hurt me, um; but even with me trying to amass everything in my mind, yet and still it came down to the bottom line, which was, I was in love with this guy and unconditionally, with all his cursing, which he knew I didn't like, but did it anyway, sometimes drinking, not being lovie dubbie as I wanted him to be, he didn't love kissing like I did, being hugged up in public, just wasn't affectionate as I wanted him to be. But yet and still I loved him totally and completely, willing and was ready to settle; knowing I wasn't going to be happy. So why was I settling? I have to keep checking myself; do you want him happily married? Or are you jealous that he didn't marry you? But what can you do to make someone marry you? Nothing! All you can do is be yourself. If you make someone marry you, it's not right or it's not legal: what did she do? Was it because of their children? Why would you marry a person just for the sake of the children, when later on down the road you end up divorced anyway? Just looking like a family on the outside, when on the inside you're not in love with that person. He had years and months to tell me, "Shun, I've made a decision, and I'm going to do this that and the other," but he didn't even think enough of me nor respected me enough to tell me; at least he could have done that. And he had the nerve to call my love a punk, if my baby was here to see this, she would die all over again, she loved him so much.

Sitting here in the hotel room I can hear voices in the room next door, seems like I heard a male's voice say something to the child, and the child began to laugh: upon hearing those sounds (trying to read my bible) I began to cry, those were the sounds I had longed to hear in my home, but now it's some where else in another home. I feel like he snatched a dream from me, a hope I had is now lost. I think of the fun we had, the laughter we gave to each other, the things he bought me, the kind deeds he did for me, how? Can some body; please help me out with this one? How can someone who say they love you so much, who makes you so happy, make you so sad and hurt you so bad?

Starting the play tonight in Greensboro, N.C. at the rehearsal before the show, one of the musicians came up to me to speak, then he asked about the player, which was limited conversation for me, anyway he concluded with, don't be mad at me, I'm just a friend of the player; then I said, I have no ill feelings towards him or his wife. I was so upset that he would approach me in that manner as if we had it like that, Mr. Player is married now and they are a family and if any one knows me, when it comes to another woman's husband or boyfriend, my hands are off. I don't play in that area. I've let God down once, twice and too many times that I care to remember and I don't plan to do it again. So the guy went on to say, "well anyway he never introduced you to us as his girlfriend, he just told us that he was your manager, period. Boy, did I feel worse; because if anything, if a guy likes you at least his boys should know who you are, or they should be able to see him taking a little more interest in you than any other woman. So I told my sister, Latrice what happened, I told her, girl I've been played like a fiddle; she said, No, he played his self, I said to her, I can see myself at the Grammies giving my acceptance speech and at my closing saying, "I would like to thank all the men (who hurt me) who were blind, with no balls, slippery hands and small pockets." (If you can't figure this out, then call me, I'll tell you later).

I just remembered, after preaching somewhere, I forgot what city, but the Bishop came up to me and said, "now that's what I'm talking about, a woman with purpose; to come here and preach in spite of what's all going on in your life, you still came and minis-tered to the people of God, and blessed us," he said, "That's what soldiers do: they keep fighting in spite of the wounds, hurts or pain; like the scripture says, Thou therefore endure hardness as a good soldier of Jesus Christ, (II Tim. 2:3)

One thing that helps me is that I often get in the mirror and tell myself the truth; girl it's your fault, you fell again, you did not obey God: get yourself together, Repent! And go on, everything is going to be alright, and you can make it; just because God said it! One man's lost, is another man's gain. But, I must admit the wall is back up again, only higher and thicker, that's what I get for falling for a sinner. If the nigga ain't saved, leave him alone, and if the hussy ain't saved, leave her alone. He told me that he had accepted Christ, but any man who does what he did, Jesus is not present, I guess my brother (Bishop M.J. Pace) was right, he told me that this guy was a merchandiser. You know, slowly but surely my feelings are changing, because the more I look at it, I was never in the picture from the beginning, I was just the 'woman in passing' but as a powerful woman of God once said to me, "nothing with God goes to waste" thank you Pastor S.C. of Oakland, Ca. But nothing good is going to come to him until he back that thing up, and do it right. No not marry me, but ask for forgiveness, to God first and then to me, because he knew that he was never going to make a commitment to me all along and for down right using me, my talent, my money and my love: to sum it up in one word, Abuse [a-buse: to use in an improper or wrong way.] To mislead an individual into thinking that you love them is abuse; to sleep with a person and you are married is abuse, to both parties, especially if one party doesn't know; to lie altogether, is abuse, (i.h.) improper handling. Pastor C. gave me another illustration of abuse, she said, "if you owned a Mercedes Benz, you wouldn't take it to a fix or repair daily place to keep it up or put any kind of gas in it, that would be abuse, but you'd take it to the best mechanic and put the best type of gas in it, the best of everything: but that's only if you know what you have". She said, "He didn't know you nor did he love you, so therefore he didn't know how to treat you, because he never knew what he had." At one point, I wanted revenge; but when I allowed God through Jesus and his Spirit, the Holy Ghost to do a work on me, those feelings are gone. I feel sorry for the persons who do others wrong, because when God gets you; you're gotten: you will wish that it was the person instead of God, because your arms are too short to box with him. Who can get God back? **NO ONE!!!!!!!!!!!!!!!!!** He can do what you can't do, and you come out smelling like a rose.

June 15, 01

Today, well this morning in my prayer time (3:00 a.m.) I noticed something strange, I didn't feel my best friend near me and I know that he's always there, um he just whispered something to me, I'll tell you later: but when I would pray to him he wouldn't say nothing back, I had been feeling alone already until just now, well what he said was, "I've been sad from the way you've been hurting." I felt special and loved. But I tell you, my heart has been ripped in more ways than a hundred, the blood just keep dripping: I saw myself on my knees with my bleeding heart in my hands, giving it to God. I'm reminded of the story in the Jabez book, how the son couldn't go up the ladder of the highest sliding board on the play ground, him knowing that he couldn't handle it called out to his daddy saying, "daddy help me, **it's too big for me.**" After reading this story I began to cry, calling out to my heavenly Father, Help! It's too big for me! God has truly made me his woman of purpose and character and strength. He is my shield and my buckler or else I would have been destroyed at the hand of the enemy and he will not suffer the righteous to be moved. Thank you Lord, I Will Bless The Lord At All Times!

Not that I haven't asked for forgiveness of my sins, and I have. But today I asked the Lord to forgive me of every sexual act I had done and to wash me clean all over again. For I will cleanse their blood that I have not cleansed: for the Lord dwelleth in Zion. (Joel 3:21) Lord, please keep me in my right mind and in your hands. By the way thank you Y. A. for your note book "The Experience" to write my daily diary, it is now the "La Shun Pace Experiences."

June 17, 01

Happy Father's Day! To God Almighty and to my Daddy. I'm having a real good day!!! Thank You Jesus! My sister and I just ordered a big breakfast here in Greensboro, it's the last day of the play. I still had a few thoughts, but they were thoughts of me doing my own play one day: I pray that the men who come to my play won't think that I'm a male basher, because I'm not. But I will be catering to the hurting women. Let's face it women, we do have a revengeful spirit, but some women have a vicious revengeful spirit, but not me, however (smile) at one point I did want all the stuff that I'd given him and all the monies I had dished out, but you know what, every dog has its day. I guess he had a lot to loose may be he was told if he'd married someone else that he wouldn't see his children as often and I know how he loves his children, and mothers weigh a lot in their sons decisions and she definitely thought that he should have married the children's Mom, she even told me herself, she said, "La Shun if she was good enough for him to sleep with her, then she's good enough for him to marry her," but whatever happened to marring for love and not convenience. But he made his choice and I have to live with that, even if he's distressed with the decision he had to make.

I can't wait to see him and find out the truth of the whole matter, please Holy Spirit, my best friend; be with me and help me to be able to handle the truth. He's in Atlanta, while I'm in North Carolina, may be that's a good thing; please lets be clear, I want nothing back from him, he owes me nothing but an explanation and he don't have to give that, my sister wants to do something, I shouldn't have told her, but I needed to vent and just talk so that I could feel better. Is it for the world to know? What if he comes back? Will I regret sharing my diary? And what about my family; will they be able to forgive him and receive him without giving him a hard time? Just thoughts going through my head, I am forgiving him each day as it comes, but is my family doing the same? How are they taking this? Because believe it or not when things like this happens it affect those around you, whom you love, because they love you. But me knowing my family, they will forgive how I know? Because they want to go to heaven.

June 19, 01

Sitting here watching the Black awards show and my heart is so sad, because by now he would have called me saying do you see this, that and the other. Look at so and so, or can you believe that? They need you on the stage to show them niggas how to sing. (Smile) Oh, my heart was missing that, we had so much fun. Every time the phone rings while watching the show, I thought it was him, and I knew it wasn't, but I was thinking that way. Yea! My girl won (no more drama) I was screaming, I could hear him saying can you believe that! She won over his singer? And I would say yes! My girl is a baaad girl, and if we were at a hotel, he would call my room and stay on the phone a while, hang up, call back, he'd do this all during the show. But like I said, before all this was snatched from me abruptly: all at once GONE! This is what's so hard and so sad about the whole thing and why I said it felt like a second death, because my daughter was taken the same way; two loves gone, back to back. Any way we'd discuss the Black awards stage, how it was, what he liked about it or what he didn't like. Then he would say, how he'd want my stages to look when I blow up and start touring on the road. He would always say to me, that I was the Best singer in the whole wide world: and that no other singer, gospel or R&B could sit in the same dug out hole with me. What great honor bestowed upon me from an earthly man.

June 24, 01

At the airport in Orange County, CA. with over an hour lay over; I've just come from Suffolk, VA. Preaching; tonight I'm in concert for the Music and Arts Love Fellowship Conference in Oakland, CA. If the Lords will, I pray that a portion of last nights anointing be greater in me tonight. Standing here in the golden arch line I saw a lady that looked like the woman he married and her eyes looked just like his mother's, the lady was short like his mother, then I said to myself, maybe that's why his mother wanted him to marry her, she looks just like them, short, light and not heavy. I'm none of the three, when I'm up ministering I tell people, don't call me fat, just call me blessed, and I'm blessed in all the right places. Well, his mother got her wish.

I'm getting better, until I think on how low down and dirty the whole thing was and how it happened. I can be in the grocery store line, the fast food line in or out of the car, just wherever and the tears would begin to fill my eyes and I'd try with everything within me to fight them back. I keep asking my best friend to ensnare me into the presence of the Almighty Father, where He only can give me full understanding of the whole matter. I keep seeing couples hugged up everywhere and now here in my hotel room I get a surprise visit from room service. Answering the door, there stood a young man holding a silver tray, very beautiful with a bottle of champagne, two glasses, a bowl of strawberries and a can of whip cream (honest to God this really happened). Then the guy said, "congratulations on your wedding, may you have many, many happy anniversaries." I stood there with this look of, is this a joke? It's so not funny: so I looked at him, then turned around, looked the room over and back at him and said you have the wrong room, and then he said, "This is room so and so, right?" I said, "Yes it is." Then he motioned to give me the tray, and I said, "Sir, first of all I didn't order room service, secondly I'm not married, you have the wrong room." He showed me the paper and true enough it had my room number on it. (So me with my warp thinking at the time) I thought it was a 'sign' from God (ha-ha) thus beginning a whole new set of emotions, feelings and questions, Lord, you think something is gonna happen and we got married after all? Or maybe he's gone leave her and then ask me to marry him. I was just stupid, silly, I'd gone crazy; but God had something waiting on me. After I came to myself I told the Lord, I don't ever want to be in another relationship again, except for me and the big three, as my daddy calls them. (The Father, The Son & The Holy Ghost.

June 25, 01

I remembered yesterday on the plane I had a dream about him, we were at the same airport, I don't recall us being on the same plane, but he was carrying about five huge blue bags and one of them was so heavy while he was pulling it, it begin to make tracks in the dirt, then he went and found this table like thing with wheels on it, put the bags on it and pushed them to wherever he was going. I asked, "What are you doing, and where are you going." He said that he was going to meet my sister Latrice with the play in Ohio. I asked the Lord, what did the dream mean. I knew my sister had gotten a phone call to do a play, but at that time she had not accepted the offer yet, so that part of the dream I understood, so I called her and told her the dream and that it meant she was going to be with the play and that she was going to see him, so be nice and kind because he may want to talk to you. Not that she was going to be nasty or anything, but a sister can be cold if she wants too. Besides I thought that he would try and get a message to me and I could find out some other stuff I wanted to know, and that he could know how I was doing.

It's about 2:34 a.m. west coast time, all at once I started crying from this so, so, sad feeling that came over me, so lonely, so very sad. I asked my best friend what was it I was feeling. But while I was crying I remembered something, a few days after I buried my daughter, I was at church and one of the brothers came to me after service and said, Sister Shun, the Lord told me to tell you that, going through the death experience of your daughter, was preparing you for something worse. With tears in my eyes, I said "Yes Lord, I receive it" Lord Help me. (I wasn't calling him Lord, that's what came out)

I had no clue, I thought someone else was going to die, or that something was going to happen to my other daughter, I didn't know what, who, or nothing. But if God said it, then He was going to keep me, was the attitude I had.

This was it. Yet trying to travel and minister to others when I'm barely hanging on myself, is sooo hard to do. There are times I asked the Lord, why am I here? And why am I going on another trip? I need to be home.

June 26, 01

Today I had lunch with the assistant Pastor of Love Center Church, while I was up ministering last night in concert, I shared my testimony. I was in tears; little did I know that the Bishop H. was watching me prayerfully, as well as Pastor C. So after church the Bishop said to Pastor C. I want you to spend some time with Shun tomorrow, she needs it. She told me that she said to him, Bishop; the Holy Spirit has already dealt with me concerning the same thing. So after my class we went to a restaurant, sat down, ordered our food and I thought we were going to eat. We ate very little; first she shared her testimony with me which was almost identical to mine. She ministered to my soul and to my spirit. The Holy Ghost through her gave me what thus said the Lord. Some things were good, and some wasn't, but I needed every thing that God had spoken to her, to give to me. From my pass, up to this present time in my life, God: through her, gave me what would have been a years worth of physic iatric counseling, God did it in about two hours. Two hurting things she said to me (well there were several) but the two that hit harder than any was, when she said "he **NEVER!** Loved you from the start, and that I was an answer to his money problems. He was never trying to get to know Shun. Then she went all the way there, yes she did. She asked me how was my relationship with my daddy? I went to bragging about how much I love him and how I call him king. She tucked her lips inward, with an "um" and said, but how was it as a little girl growing up? I broke into tears, all of those old feelings of hurt flooded my soul, thinking about the names he use to call us and how deep it really hurt me inside. I wanted my daddy to talk sweet to me and not yell. I wanted him to hug me and tell me I was pretty. Then she said to me "you're yet looking for the love of your daddy.

The attention and acceptance, I had longed for from my daddy, I now was looking for it through other men, because I never got it when I was a little girl. Ouch! She didn't have to go there, but yes she did. I forgot that we were in a public place and I didn't care, I needed help, quick, fast and in a hurry. She said to me "I've got to hurt you in order to help you; I was snotting all over the place. She said, he used you and he did it on purpose, he smelled what type of woman you were, he knew exactly what he was doing. Then she said, you need to grow up in a hurry from this situation, learn the lesson, repent and move on: and that God, was going to deal with him, and that she felt sorry for him because he touched you and He said to touch not mine anointed: I Chr.16:22. She said "he abused you" then she said something to me so powerful and profound, which was, but **NOTHING!** With God: goes to waste. There's nothing in your life you've done or nothing that has happened to you so bad, that God won't take it and use it for **His Glory**, and make it work out for **Your Good**.

The next day when she saw me, she said "girl you've gotten two shades lighter. All that day, people were saying how good I looked. Every since that day and even now, that's all I hear, "girl you look GOOD! And I'd say thank you very much, but on the inside saying "Thank You Jesus and Holy Spirit, best friend. Thank God for Bishop and Pastor C.

She said that the husband God has for me, is going to want nothing but me. And all the hurt that I've gone through, God said for me to write it down and don't leave out anything, for in doing this, it would be therapeutic for me and would complete the healing in me and that it was going to be a blessing to women everywhere. I then prayed, saying to God, that if he'd just touch one, I would be grateful and thankful.

June 28, 01
Oakland, CA. 3:00 a.m.

Going back to my childhood, lets deal with that. Working along beside my daddy, whom I absolutely adored and looked up to. We're down stairs in the basement, he was building a cabinet for somebody and I was helping him by passing the nails, or sanding the wood and would help put the finished product onto the back of his mid sixties early seventy blue & white truck. We had some good times on the back of that truck, me, my sisters and my brother, we would sing all the way to wherever we were going, the smallest ones had to sit up front in the cab part of the truck with mother and daddy. We also had a yellow Rambler, in the back on the left passenger side, was a hole in the floor, covered up with a piece of thin plank wood, but no one ever got hurt, God was good to us. Anyway as I would help my daddy, I'd mess up sometimes, and then he would yell at me, calling me one of the names he would use, sending me out the basement, in the dark, back into the house. Then he would say after I'd left, but I still heard him; saying "you can't do nothing right, I can't have nothing for yall! Oh how these words would hurt my feelings, I'd go to bed crying, other times this would happen, I'd go somewhere by myself and listen to my old music box, sucking my thumb, rocking myself to sleep, or I'd go sit in my special spot and watch the air planes come in for landing, or taking off. The planes were so close to our home until we had a crack in the sealing from the dinning room to the kitchen, from the vibration of the noise from the planes, but it didn't seem to bother us a bit, I guess we were use to it. But the hurting never left, from a little girl, up until I was married and to this present time. I have always wanted the approval of my daddy, I wanted to hear him say, "girl you're such a big help to me," On Easter I wanted him to say how pretty I looked; my mother always said these things but I was a daddy's girl, so if he said it then that was the last word, that said now you're somebody. So now that I'm a grown woman, I'm yet looking for a man to approve me and say nice things to me. When the first man came along saying and doing these things, I married him. It was during those years I realized how deep those words were in me, because when my love would do something wrong or something I didn't like, I would call him those same names my daddy called me. But since this last hurt with Mr. Player, I have asked my best friend to help me and heal me completely, through and through. Father in the name of Jesus! Break the cycle of looking for approval from the arms of a fleshly man. God approves me and He Loves me like no other and I LOVE HIM!!!!!!

The way I feel right now, I don't want to love anyone else, because I feel like I would be tricked, fooled and hurt again. I do no trust myself: Father, Jesus and Holy Spirit, I give my whole self to you and I heavily depend on you and trust you. I'm frail now, so Holy Spirit please hide me from myself and the evil ones, keep me under the shadow of your wings, I don't wanna come out.

In the midst of my crying today, my best friend said to me, "look at him; let me show you something," he brought his face before me and said, "what do you see?" said the Holy Spirit and he started revealing and uncovering the truth.

(1) a person who never repented of his sins.
(2) a person who don't know God.
(3) a person who didn't love God.
(4) a person who didn't have a relationship with God (a prayer life).
(5) a person who didn't pay tithes or offerings (consistently).
(6) a liar
(7) a manipulator
(8) a merchandiser.
(9) a killer of my spirit and eventually my soul.

This was what the Holy Spirit showed me. He also jogged my memory when I was with Pastor C. hearing her say that the enemy through this last person wanted to render me helpless and powerless to my ultimate destruction. But God said, "Not so!" She said girl the devil hates it when you wake up each morning, because he knows the work you must do and the anointing you have which shall destroy his plans and his works. Father, God Almighty! I thank you for sparing my life and not cutting me off in my sins, now I can complete my course and fight the good fight of faith until you catch me up to Heaven (home).

June 29, 01 3:55 p.m.

This evening at rehearsal another musician who knew about the situation said that he felt bad about what happened and that the guy should have been man enough to tell me. What I heard two years ago was true, he told somebody that he was never going to marry me. My mother told me to let him go, but I wouldn't, so face it girl, you should have obeyed.

- My mother also told me to leave him alone, I wouldn't
- I was warned by my god mother of Illinois, who told me that things would work out if I don't compromise, I did.
- My other god mother of Memphis told me to guard my heart, I didn't.
- So face it girl, you pay for your mistakes.

June 30, 01

This morning 3:43 a.m. waking up with him on my mind going to the bathroom (the Holy Spirit just whispered something to me), my thoughts were, and you gave him a key to your first apartment and to your car. Now I thought I was a pretty level headed girl, but when I thought that he was going to pop the question any day now. Thinking this is it, he's the one. I got crazy and just lost all my senses, these items aren't any good now. But I was just thinking how foolish I was, how stupid I was, girl what was wrong with you? So after getting back into bed thoughts were yet there and me being tired of it said softly, "you demons who keep bringing these thoughts to my mind, I dare you. I bind you in the name of Jesus and I cast you out of my mind and my thoughts. I plead the blood of Jesus over me right now. WOW! I felt so good.

This is what was whispered to me, the Holy Spirit said, "the reason you are being plagued by these demons is because you're not going to bed with a praise nor waking up with a praise." In other words I wasn't talking to my best friend, the Holy Ghost. When all the time I was allowing these spirits to torment me with thoughts that were negative and not good for my (s)pirit or (S)pirit. But, if I would only PRAISE! Him, all that is unholy and impure has to leave, because of the presence of the Lord. So I stopped right then and gave Him glory and Praise and Thanksgiving.

You know what? My best friend told me to do something yesterday that blew my mind, he said, "Thank me for the sin you did. Thank me for you hurting me and letting me down. Thank me for the 'so stupid' things you did for him," seems strange hu? I know, but he said to me, "I said for you to give Thanks in everything and for all things." So I started thanking him for everything and for all things from a child even up to this present time, **LORD I THANK YOU!**

You know what that did for me?

1 it made me love the Father, the Son and the Holy Spirit more. (Luke 7:47)
2 the Spirit of obedience enters into your spirit. (Acts 5:29)

3 all demons and negative spirits leave. (I Sam. 16: 23)

4 it lifts you to a place of praise, joy, peace and thanksgiving. (Ps. 63:5-6)

5 it brings you into the presence of God. (Ps. 22:3)

6 you get a spirit of compassion for others. (Gal. 6:1)

7 it sanctifies your atmosphere. (Ps. 68:1-2)

8 you appreciate the mercy of God on you life. (Lam. 3:22)

When I see him I'm going to say, Thank You. And yes, I can and will Love again, said my best friend. Then he said to me, "you never were 'in love' with him, because you loved him more than you loved me, and that's not the way you are suppose to love no one. So my child what you thought you had for him was false, My love won't hurt you." I said, "Thank you Father for loving me through your Son Jesus and you Spirit, the Holy Ghost, my best friend. And so I'm going back to sleep, but this time with a Praise, reading my bible (the words of the Lord God Almighty) and my book by M. K. B.

10:47 a.m. the same morning

Up from my morning rest again. In Georgia it's almost 2:00 p.m. which is the real time I get up anyway, g.s.t.(Gospel singers time) (smile). Oh, what a great day! He wasn't on my mind when I got up. Thank You Jesus! Also I took a look in the mirror as I was using the bathroom and I began to cry, not about my daughter Xenia nor about the guy who hurt me. But because I saw a Powerful Woman of God getting ready to be used by The Almighty God Himself. I told my best friend, this time these tears are for me. The New Me! I laughed and cried at the same time, I felt glad and joy for where Jesus and my best friend is taking me. Thank You Jesus! Thank you Jesus! Thank You Jesus!!! **I'm FREE!** Jesus the Son of God has set me free indeed.

July 1, 01

At the airport again, O.C.Ca. on my way home. Talking on the phone with one of my sisters, I feel a little bit bad, only when I heard her voice, because she's experiencing a few things of her own. I'm on the airplane in Dallas, TX. Trying to get home to my baby girl who misses me so much and I'm missing her. Our flight was delayed for over two hours, now I won't get home until around two o'clock in the a.m. So I called to let her know and to see how she was doing, then she wanted to know how I was doing. It's only been four months since we lost Xenia, our responses were the same, Okay. We both are being carried by the Spirit of God, trying to go on, but yet hurting at the same time and I'm trying to keep praising God so that I won't think about him. It's a challenge to your will. "Ouch" these pants are pinching me, I've had them on all day, time to breath down there (smile). Anyway, I'm yet dealing with the words, "he never loved you, he lied to you, he used you, etc." The Spirit spoke to me about a fast, it will be the longest one I've been on. He spoke it once in church and then in California, but we will see. We're getting ready to take off, so gotta go.

July 7, 01

Reading my word, in the book of Psalm the entire 124th book; but the verses that started me to crying was verses 7 and 8; "Our soul is escaped as a bird out of the snare of the fowler: the snare is broken and we are escaped. Our help is in the name of the Lord, who made heaven and earth." The snare **IS** Broken from A to Z, before, after and everything in between. Thus said the Holy Ghost, my best friend.

5:00 o'clock p.m. my sister Melonda, just kissed me on my right jaw at home, she don't do that, so that's why I'm taking this special moment out to write it down. This was July 17, 01

July 20, 01

Last night my sister, Latrice called me, she's with the play; yes, he's there with her. She said that he came up to her asking if the two of them needed to talk. Why would he ask that? When he already know she has questions. When you know that you've done wrong don't ask if, just talk. At times I ask myself, why you yet want somebody who's hurt you so bad. If he hurt you once, he'll do it again. I can hear the song in my spirit, "I just can't give up now, I've come to far from where I started from, nobody told me the that road would be easy. But I know and believe he didn't bring me this far to leave me."

July 21, 01

I had a wedding to do last Saturday and today looking at television another wedding. I just can't seem to get the picture of him and her standing at the alter exchanging wedding vows to each other. Then hearing the preacher say you may now kiss the bride. Or I _____ take thee _____to be my awful, lawful bla, bla, bla. And with this ring, I thee wed. I just want to cry, my hurt heart bleeds, but you know what, all this boils down to, is that he said all these things to some one else and not me. I think this is the real problem with some of us women who is experiencing the same thing, is getting over the thought of it wasn't me, it was someone else. Which could make a person feel like, I wasn't good enough or something's wrong with me, did he really do this to me, and why? And you have to come to grips with yourself and say, Yes! He did do it and he done it to me, and Yes! He married someone else. Keep saying it, now breathe and say it again. But Lord, he married someone else. I feel like one sick puppy and one sick chick, but I'm going to be alright, as long as you stay honest with yourself about everything.

I've always heard that things happen in threes, first the news of being a diabetic, then the death of my daughter and the marriage of the man I thought was mine. I still love him and wish that he'd get a divorce and marry me. So, I began to Praise God and bless his Holy name to keep my mind off the wrong thoughts, that isn't His will for my life. For his will for me, is to have my own husband and not someone else's. (I Cor. 7:2) So, I asked my best friend to take me into the presence of God and then my mind was at peace as well as my spirit, soul and body. I truly do love the Lord and I know along with time that he is going to completely heal me from all this hurt and pain, and he's going to one day use all these things to bring Him Glory and Honor. This is what I want, God is Awesome!

July 23, 01

I just seen another wedding on TV. I now pronounce you Man and Wife, or Husband and Wife. Why do I want to be married again? Is this what you really want? Some times yes and a lot of times no. Anyway, he told my sister that he needed to talk, so they got together and he said that he feel bad about what happened, so much was going wrong, so marring his children's Mom seemed like the right thing to do.. He went on to say that he misses me like F_____, Did he miss me or that? I experienced things that I didn't experience while I was married. NO! I'm not bragging or boasting about anything because sin is sin and God hates sin. Not me, but the sin I did. Nor am I condoning what happened, but God yet shows us Mercy and Love. I have asked the Lord to forgive me and I believe he has. Thank You Jesus, for your blood.

Anyway, he said more, like he didn't know what happened, everything went so fast. He told her that they argue all the time and that he wake up some mornings wondering what the ____ has he done. And the only thing he doesn't regret is putting his children to bed at night, going on school trips and taking them to the park, things like that. He told my sister that he got tired of coming home to an empty apartment, and when he would go visit his children he got tired of them asking when he was coming home. Which raised a question in my head, were they married all along? Because if he wasn't then, that wasn't home. She told me that the show was coming to Atlanta and he told her to tell me that he wants to see me; she said that she told him, Shun isn't going to see you. He asked, why? She said, because you're married, and to shun that means hands off, do not touch. Then he said to her, "I'll see". I'm on the phone with her all this time and driving at the same time. I got caught up in the conversation, going right all the time, but some how I thought I was going wrong so I turned around, I did this about three times. I had to stop, get myself together and then continue on, boy did he have me twisted all up. I wondered what he did with all the stuff I gave him down through the years; a Rolex watch, a huge down payment on his Explorer, a lot of money has been through my hands to his. But I always gave God his first and then took care of my children.

Some time in July, 01

My emotions have been on a roller coaster. Thinking he's coming to town. Someone at school called my baby fat, which made me think of my daughter Xenia and how she was treated at school. Now the same thing is happening with Aarion. Should I talk to him when he comes? If I ask for advice, will the answer be no? I really do want to talk to him, but I don't want anybody to know, because they won't understand. How is his mother doing? How could he be so heartless? He used me, all these things were going on in my head. Lord, I don't want another relationship with anything that has a penis. And, no I'm not a lesbian. I'm just tired of all the drama, the games and the lies. This one really took me for a loop. I'm still caught somewhere in one of the O's or the left corner of the L. I'll just let you pick a letter it doesn't matter, I'm in there somewhere. I know that if there's a beginning then there's an ending, but the truth is I don't want to come out too quick, only when I'm ready and then, like I said, I just don't want to be bothered, getting to know a person, spending time, energy and effort, boy it's draining.

I must admit, that I was glad to hear that they weren't getting along, but then I thought about their children and them having to hear mommy and daddy fussing. My daughter Xenia went through that and you don't want to see that kind of hurt on your child's face, it disturbs their peace and their emotions, imagine what it's doing to their hearts. I'm angry, because I told him once that getting married for the sake of the children is NEVER! the solution to any couples problems who have children or a child together, because the end results will always be bad. And Children have enough to deal with besides their parents ending up in divorce court, divorce is a killer. And not just of the couples, but the children, families involved and friends. And in the words of my mother, when she spoke at my daughter's home going. She told the men that if they 'keep peter in the gate', meaning keep your stuff zipped up in you pants and only take it out for **your WIFE!** Then what we are going through today won't have to happen. And I'm saying to the single women tell the man in your life, first of all if he's saved he shouldn't be asking you to sleep with him, but if it comes up; tell him 'No Wedding Ring, NO Dickaling'. And to the married women 'the honey in your hive, is for one bee'. **Your husband.**

May, 02

It's been almost a year now from the time I got the news; I finally heard from him, it was abut 4:00 a.m. I'm usually up praying, but this time I was sleep. The phone rung and I saw his name on the ID, I said hello, he said Shun and I called his name, he said I miss you man, I love you and I said I miss you and I love you too. But I have a few questions for you that only you can answer. He said shoot. I said okay, how could you get married and not tell me? How could you hurt me like that? How could you come to the funeral of my daughter acting like you cared knowing that within four days you were getting married? Why were you in my life all these years? Do you remember when we were in VA? And I asked you what were your intentions of being in my life and I asked you then were you going to marry me, and you said that you weren't proposing marriage right now? Do you remember in Italy when I asked you the same question and you said to me that if God said that you were my husband, then I should let go and let God? Do you remember again me asking what are you here in my life for and you answered, I'm here for the long haul? I just need to know why? So that I can bring closure to this book. He begin to explain, when he finished, I said, you could have married me for the reasons you just named; talking about he was lonely, (then marry me and live with me), he needed money (I was giving you that), he was missing his children (we could go visit or let them stay with us sometimes). I started thinking and said to myself, girl you've been there, done this, you don't wanna go there again, so I just listened to all his excuses but, my bucket had no bottom, so all his excuses fell straight to the ground. I said you called me a while back telling me how you wanted to tell me what went down, how it happened and all the particulars. I'm yet waiting, I confronted him about some one seeing him in a hallmark store picking up wedding invitations, which takes time to order and the honeymoon package my travel agent set up for him, who told my booking person, who told my sister, who told me and that's how I found out. I'm yet waiting, he had no explanation, real or fake; witchcraft or not, no one forced him to marry her. I told him, let me show you what you did; I told him, you had to have thought about this thing. You said, if I marry my children's mom, it's going to hurt Shun, and if I marry Shun, then my children's mom will be hurt and do this that and the other, so you in your right mind made a choice and said; okay, I'll hurt Shun and that's what you did. He said, "I know what I did was wrong, but I have asked the Lord to forgive me, and I hope that you can do the same." I replied, "If I hadn't, I wouldn't be on this phone talking to you now." But I let him hear me say I forgive you and yet love you, but not the way I use to. I explained to him that the kind of love I had for him; that only God Almighty could take away. I told him I didn't just love him, I reverenced him, because when you love someone and all of a sudden you hear that they're married, it takes God to deal with you, where you are, reestablishing and renewing your mind, bringing me to this place where I am now. I then begin to minister to him about now that he's repented and got things right with the Lord that he needs to be the spiritual leader of his household, pay tithes and offerings faithfully, pray for and with your children and his wife. Love her and do right by her. You know what he did; he asked me if he could come down and see me. I said, "No!" He asked why not, I said you're married, he said I just want to see you face to face. I said you don't have to see me, you can say whatever it is you need to say right here over the phone. He said I'm coming anyway, I said come on and I'll be gone, and went back to ministering to him, asking him if I could pray with him before I hung up and he said, no, that's alright. then I thought, "he's on the phone, I wonder where he is," so I asked him, "where are you?" "in the car," he said. I asked, where's your wife, he said at a conference. I said so why are you not at home. He said he just felt like riding. I said um,um then he said, Oh no, I don't have to sneak around and call you, I can call you from the house; I said right. The last time you called me someone broke out the window of your car and stole your cell phone. Please! Anyway, we hung up and about twenty minutes later he called back. I said, "hello", he was trying to sound sexy; I said sternly, "hello, I can't hear you," then he cleared his throat and repeated himself which was, what are you thinking? I said, about you calling me and for what reason. Then he said, "well I've accomplished my first step", I said, "how many steps do you have?" he began to laugh saying, "I don't know," then he did his famous thing of rushing me off the phone as if he's so busy or just have to go some where urgently, so I said, bye and went back to sleep. To this day I don't think of him hardly ever, Thank You Jesus.

July, 02

He called again about three months ago around his birthday, just checking on me so he said; to se how I was doing. Also asking me if I didn't mind him traveling with me again from time to time, but it was totally up to me, he said that he was just throwing it out there and that the decision was up to me; and I said, you're right and left it at that. I asked how was his mother doing? He said not good, she was going through a few rough times, she had lost a love one as well. I said for him to tell her she's in my prayers. I asked how he and his wife and children were? He said their alright, then he asked about Aarion, I said that she had a cold and that my mother was taking her to the doctor that day, he wished her well, then there was silence; this happened about twice while we were on the phone, reason; I knew I had nothing much to say, conversation was limited, he said, I hope you don't get your number changed like you did last time, I said, that was then, this is now and it ain't that deep any more. I had no reason to do that and he could call as many times as he wanted. Then he started asking about my family, my niece and nephews, just everybody. So after he was finished asking about everybody it got quiet again, so this time my best friend said to me, you remember all the times he rushed you off the phone, I said yes, he said now rush him off. He didn't have to tell me twice, I said well Player, I gotta go, my mother is waiting on me to bring Aarion. He started saying something, I couldn't quite get it, because I was saying okay, tell your mother I said hello, have a good day, bye, bye and hung up the phone. YES! Laughing all the way to my Mom's house. Like the song says, some how the wires have crossed, the tables are turned........I've got a new attitude.

Ladies if he's married, he's off limits according to the word of God and the Law. (I Cor. 7:2) Nothing and nobody is worth you loosing your soul. (Matt. 16:26). For the devil comes to steal, kill and destroy; but Jesus came to give us life more abundantly. (John 10:10). I Thank God for keeping me from all three; I had gone through so much and the pressure was great. My hair fell out, my love even took me back to court to tell the judge I killed my daughter, and the man I loved married on me; under all of this and having to yet travel, then I had to go home and be a full time mother; I was about to loose it; "But God." Reading my bible one day in the hotel room, I fell off to sleep, but my best friend woke me up and said, start reading your bible, again I was puzzled, because I had just finished reading. So I got up, picked up the bible and started reading where I had left off and while I was reading a sharp pain hit me, from the corner of my left eye up through the middle of the mid top of my head; this pan was so sharp and hard until it closed my left eye completely, but I heard my best friend say, KEEP READING! And with that one eye closed, I continued to read. When the pain had gone, I sat on the side of the bed saying Lord what was that? I had never experienced nothing like that; later on I had to use the bathroom and while there the Holy Ghost said to me, "I just spared you from a aneurysm", I forgot about where I was and I danced like a crazy woman, giving God Thanks. I danced until I was out of breath, then I went prostrate on the floor to worship him. I called my mother as soon as I could and told her what the Lord had done and what he had said, she started speaking in tongues, then she said, "Shun, I believe it because of all you've gone through and ain't no telling what else he's kept you from." Before going to church that night my best friend shared something else with me, he said to me, "you are a Praiser, a Worshipper and a Dancer," he said, "you Praise me for what I've done, you worship me for who I am, and you Dance because of what you know." Before these things occurred in my life, I was s sometime saint; I would read God's word sometimes; I would fast and pray, sometimes; I would obey God, sometimes. It is because God allowed these things to happen in my life, that I have drawn closer to him, within seven months I read the entire bible from Genesis to Revelation. I thought I had did something, I started telling it in my testimony until one day my best friend said to me, you think you've done such a wonderful thing, how long have you been saved? He asked me, and I said for such and such years; he said and you're just now reading my word all the way through. He ripped me so sweetly, all I could feel was shame. He brought to my attention how I'd read other books and novels, sometimes one book twice: he said to me all those times in your life when you wanted to take your life, it was because you didn't have

NO! word in you and all those times you were depressed and felt like backsliding. You didn't have NO! word in you, all these times you were slipping in and out of sin. You didn't have NO! word in you; and every time the devil and his demons came to your mind with mess and junk and you gave in to it. YOU didn't have NO! word in you; then he started quoting to me the scriptures, that if I hide the word in my heart: I won't sin. If I thought on things lovely, pure, good reports, things that are true, and honest…, Not to give place to the devil: and that if I keep my mind stayed on Him(the word), he would keep me in perfect peace; Resist the devil and he would flee; My best friend went on and on, I was like; Okay! Already, I believe I got it, but he didn't stop there. He called me a weekend shacker, he said you know what you were no better than people who shack, you were just doing your thang on the weekend. I said, OH! My God, Ouch! Now that lick hurt; he broke it on down to me, he said if you're sharing a bed, not living quarters, but a bed with a man and you are not married to him, you're shacking: ain't no sweet way to put it. But just like a best friend, after telling you (off) about your self, they build you up by letting you know, it's all good. He told me to read the bible and it opened to this scripture automatically; and when I read the last five words all I could do was cry, because God is so merciful to me/us. In spite of ourselves; that's why I sing the song, "he keeps on doing great things for me," "God has smiled on me, he has set me free, God has smiled on me he's been good to me:" let me give ya'll this scripture before I get happy! Up in here, up in here.

If God has set you free, gave you the Victory; you got a right to Praise Him, go ahead; get yo praise on. and Tell It!

And the Scribes and the Pharisees brought unto him a woman taken in (sin) adultery: and when they had set her in the midst, they say unto him, Master, this woman was taken in adultery, in the very act. Now Moses in the law commanded us, that such should be stoned: but what sayest thou? This they said, tempting him that they might have to accuse him. But Jesus stooped down, and with his finger wrote on the ground, as though he heard them not. So when they continued asking him, he lifted up himself, and said unto them, He that is without sin among you, let him first cast a stone at her.

And again he stooped down and wrote on the ground. And they which heard it being convicted by their own conscience went out one by one, beginning at the eldest even unto the last: and Jesus was left alone, and the woman standing in the midst. When Jesus had lifted up himself, and saw none but the woman, he said unto her, Woman, where are those thine accusers? Hath no man condemn thee? She said, No man, Lord. And Jesus said unto her, Neither do I condemn thee: **go and sin no more.** (St. John 8:3-11)

May 5, 03

My sister, Latrice is at my house, we're at the table playing scrabble and eating lunch. When she said, "girl player is something else, he was talking to me on line the other day, he wanted to know how you were doing, and he told me to tell you, to tell your best friend he can ease up now." (he was referring to the Holy Ghost) I laughed and said, "I can't tell him what to do as for him reaping what he's sown, but I do pray for him and his wife and children that God keep them together and make them one." Then I said for her to tell him, "I pray my best friend get him until he comes completely to him". So the next day she called me, because they had talked again on line and he wanted her to ask me if he could have my number, he just wanted to talk to me. I had the phone on speaker phone so the others in the house heard, when Phyllis yelled out, "No Shun, No." Then I said to Latrice, "No he can't have my number because I don't want his wife to think that I have feelings for her husband any more and No because I feel its wrong. If I was the wife I wouldn't want him calling the other woman." But I did understand if the script was flipped, because after all he would have to stay in touch with his children as a daddy. Anyway I didn't give her a yes or a no, I told her that if I decided to talk to him, some people may not understand. I did want to talk to him but not by phone, again. I needed to see this man face to face. I wanted to see his expression when I asked him why did he do it. (no it was not going to matter, because he is married and that's that). But it's like I've heard people say, "you need to face your demons," for then you will truly know where you stand, and it will really tell the truth.

Not seeing him for over two and a half years, only talking over the phone a few times. Not seeing some one for that length of time, love does go away with the help of the Holy Ghost (my best friend), or maybe I should say being in love, you yet love but not at the same level. To sum up what I'm trying to say. It's a whole new ball game when you see an old flame face to face, because old feelings can be rekindled. So all this talk of me being totally healed, delivered and over him; seeing him would be the real true test.

May 9, 03

I'm in Connecticut for a week I'm the guest Psalmist for the CCC convocation. Churches Connected Covenant Convocation.

May 15, 03

My cell phone rings again, I see the number and thought it was my friend M.Q.M. but it was Mr. Player. I had told him I would be in Connecticut. After answering the phone, he wanted to know why wasn't my phone on earlier, because he wanted to come see me and couldn't reach me. I just said, okay. But in my mind I was saying, "how you, being married, gone come almost two hours away and see me without your wife knowing where you are." He must have heard my thoughts because he said he had nothing to hide, he and his wife speak of me often. I said, "O really". He said he would tell her of some things that happen funny on the road when he was my manager. But I couldn't help thinking that they were laughing at me and not with me. Anyway, he said M. Q. M. emailed him, letting him know I would be at a church in his hood to sing May 17, 03. But he said he would try to come see me if he could, because he had a game with his little league at 7:30 and the concert started at 7:00. So I said, "if you can make it fine, if not I understand." He said on the other hand it's supposed to rain. I was like, okay whatever; it would be good to see you, but if not it's okay. Then he said, "what time will you get over here Saturday," I said, "we (me and my BB) plan to get there early, because she want to see New York." Then he said, "Good, if you get in early then maybe we'll get a chance to see each other." I said, "Maybe so." Today is Friday and as my god daddy says, 'tomorrow we will see the conclusion of these matters.

May 17, 03

'Ring, Ring, Ring, Ring', "Hello", "what took you so long to answer the phone." " I just heard the ring." "oh! Okay so where are you?" " I'm at the church," "you're at the church right now?" "yea," "stay right there, I'll be there in two minutes," "alright." The happiness I heard in his voice was indescribable. He came speeding up beside the parked car I was in, when we looked at each other, I knew God had set me free and he knew it too. He asked if I would step out of the car so we could talk, at first I said no, then I retracted and said sure lets talk. We sat on the steps of the church. I told him I needed to see him face to face to see if God had delivered me. So he asked if any thing was still there, and I said very peacefully and calmly, "no it's gone." This gave me the opportunity to see his face as I asked him why did he do it. And the bottom line was 'he did it for his children'. Then I said, "the final reason I wanted to see you was to apologize face to face and ask you to forgive me, because I don't want you to think that all church women would do what I did; what hurt me the most was how I let God down." And I asked again, "will you forgive me". He said, "yes, will you forgive me". We forgave each other. Then I told him he could not call me any more. It looked as if his chest was about to burst and his eyes got teary. Trying to explain why he could not call me any more, I asked him did he understand, he replied, "no". I said I am not trying to hurt you, because it's not about you, it's about your wife; I respect her as a woman, wife and a mother, because I can identify with all three. The first reason was because it was wrong; the second, you reap what you sow. His response was, " well if I never see you again, just know that I loved you and I love you and will always love you." He also said, " he thinks of me 22 hours of the day." (But my best friend whispered to me, "I think of you 24") all I could do was smile when the Holy Ghost told me that. Long story short, I told him I had to go, he said, "he wasn't ready to leave yet," I said, "you can stay here, you left the first time, now allow me this time to leave first." I walked off and never looked back, knowing that God had given me the Victory over, 'he didn't marry me'. Oh what a bitter ending, for a sweet new beginning.

My Affirmation Prayer

As given to me by the Holy Spirit, my best friend

Father in the name of Jesus, I ask that your Spirit, the Holy Ghost Himself, would make intercession for me, and bring this my prayer into the throne room where your presence reveals all and removes all that is unholy and impure. Father, I confess all the sins of my past. Every thing that I have ever done, that wasn't in your will, or your plan. I ask for your forgiveness of every sexual act of any kind, Lord sanctify my spirit, mind, soul, body and my will, holy and wholly unto you. I come to you in all and with all my brokenness and my wounded spirit and my crippled soul. I confess my feelings of hatred, bitterness, anger and revengefulness and all unholy and impure thoughts of the ones who hurt me or caused me pain. Holy Spirit, take me now into the presence of The Almighty God: where only He can remove all the pain, grief and hurt, I lay my head on your bosom Father, love the hurt away.

Father, I read in your word where you said, that in your presence is the fullness of joy; and David said, to let God arise: and my enemies would be scattered and be driven away like smoke and would melt like wax to fire, only at your presence. I now pray for your presence, Almighty Father to forever, always be in my life. Father in the name of your son Jesus, keep my spirit in your presence, so that when men see me, they will see you being glorified through your son Jesus, in my life. Father I pray that when I leave your presence, I will not leave the same way I came. All my brokenness is made whole, all my hurts and wounds are healed, and all internal sickness or illness is made completely whole, all sickness and disease of any kind, spiritual, physically, emotionally, mentally and financially, is made whole in the powerful, precious Name of Jesus the Christ, the son of the living God Amen. *Please take a few moments right here, lift up your hands in the presence of God: and began to Praise Him and Thank Him, for what he's done, now as you Praise him, release every person who has hurt you.*

Daddy, brother, cousin, nephew, mother, sister, friend, uncle, stranger, Pastor, husband, in-laws, niece, teacher, co-worker, boss, church folk, etc. RELEASE them into the hands of your best friend, The Holy Ghost, whatever they did, or said ask the Holy Spirit to take it, here I give it to you. And now Father, I thank you for giving me beauty for ashes, the oil of joy

for morning, the garment of praise for the spirit of heaviness: that I might be called a tree of righteousness, the planting of the Lord, that He might be glorified.

Holy Spirit now teach me how to love myself and see myself the way my heavenly Father sees me. I confess, that I can not buy a mans love, but I can give love, whether it's returned to me or not. I am a woman/man of Gods purpose, I will not be distracted, or loose my focus, for I know and the enemy knows that, in the hands of God: I am a Powerful Weapon! Ready to be used of God; to fight spiritual warfare in the kingdom of my Father, God Almighty: to win souls for His kingdom, in the Name of Jesus Christ.

I confess I am made by God: fearfully and wonderfully, He created me in his own Image; not to be used or abused by a man or a woman, I belong to God and I am complete in Him alone. I am a Beautiful Woman/Handsome Man full of life, because the life giver lives on the inside of me. I am more than a conqueror through Christ Jesus who loves me. Holy Spirit, don't let the hurts of my pass cause me to not love again, just help me from this point on to acknowledge you in all my ways and in all the affairs of my life.

I trust you Lord, for in this I am blessed. Thank you for making me a vessel of Honor, I love you Lord; with all my soul, with all my heart, with all my might and with all my strength. I come to you with all honesty, bearing the precious blood of your son Jesus Christ, the only begotten of the Father, and with the anointing you have given me.

[Now Father in the Name of Jesus, and by your Spirit, the Holy Ghost; I ask that you break every curse off these men, women, children, homes, and families, ten generations back and ten to come, we break the curse of low self esteem, pity, shame, perversion, and all other spirits I cannot name, Holy Spirit intercede now on our behalf. Satan the LORD rebuke you, and Lord we Thank You for total deliverance in Jesus Name.

Lord; open my Spiritual eyes to see men by their spirits, and not the outward flesh. This affirmation prayer I pray, confess and believe in Jesus Name Amen, and it is So!!!

Things I hold on to

Feb. 28,01 A few days after Xenia's home going service, I was at the hotel with Phyllis (auntie mommy) and the phone rung, the room was packed with family, talking and laughing, but I could still hear my mother on the phone talking to the person on the other end, when I heard her say "Shun, yes she's here". I got the phone and to my surprise it was my nephew calling from incarceration, to see how every one was doing especially me and Aarion. He said to me "Auntie you are a strong woman," and I said, "no I'm not," but he insisted, saying yes you are. He told us that he was watching TV and saw what had happened to his cousin, Xenia. I said to him, "I wondered if you knew." Then he said to me that the Lord had given him something to tell me, but he didn't know how he was going to get the message to me, and I was there the very moment he called. He said, "auntie, first of all I want you to know that I'm in here with men who has done all kind of things to their children, and the Lord said, one of the reasons he took Xenia was that she was about to encounter something that none of us would have been able to handle," And that he (the Lord) loved me too much to see me go through that kind of hurt and pain, so he took her. Then he continued by saying, no auntie she had not been molested, but it was about to happen. (He shall redeem their soul from deceit and violence: Ps. 72:14a). Thank God for sparing me !!! because ya'll know, that the rest of my days would have been spent doing prison ministry, from the inside, (smile). No I may not have killed the person, but I would have paid someone to do it for me, now I know that it sounds bad, but I'm just keeping it REAL and telling ya'll the truth. I believe that the Lord told my nephew what he told me, because number one he wasn't there when the Lord said to me, "I took her," and he quoted these words verbatim, secondly he wasn't there when Xenia said to me at MDT, about how she didn't like certain things that was done to her, I know some of you may say, how can God speak to someone behind bars? First of all he's in there because of bad decisions, so now he's suffering the consequences. But God can speak through anyone He chooses. If he can speak through a donkey; [and the Lord opened the mouth of the ass, and she said unto balaam, what have I done unto thee, that thou has smitten me these three times? And the ass said unto Balaam..Num. 22:28 – 30] he definitely can speak through man. So I hold on to the fact of knowing that God spared Xenia, me and the rest of my family from destruction.

I hold on to knowing that she is with the Lord, [For WE know that if our earthly house of this tabernacle were dissolved, we have a building of God an house not made with hands, eternal in the heavens. We are confident, I say, and will rather to be absent from the body and to be present with the Lord. II Cor. 5:1& 8] and Ps. 116:15 reads; Precious in the sight of the Lord is the death of his saints.

I hold on to all of the precious memories and photos down through the years, I hold on to her beautiful smile, which made her cheeks rise like two suns in the morning, her soft spoken voice saying, "I love you mommy." I hold on to her laughter and the love she had for me, our talks of her giving me advice and even sometimes consoling me, Oh! The precious memories; how they linger. I happily hold on to forever having her voice recorded singing with me on my CD "God is Faithful." (song, A mothers prayer)

From the moment of me knowing that I was with child, to the very last day, that I dropped her off at school and gave her, her last hug and kiss, that I will forever HOLD ON TO.

BUT THE MAIN THING I HOLD ON TO IS THE WORD OF God and his love for me, for he knows all. I am the Alpha and

Omega, the beginning and the ending, saith the Lord, which is and which was and which is to come, the Almighty. [Rev. 1:8]

Are you surrounded by people like Job had around him, at times? Job felt like the words that his friends were speaking wasn't helping his situation, so he said to them; how long will you vex my soul and break me in pieces with "words". [Job 19:2] {**W O R D S!** They can build you up or tare you down; they can make you smile or make you frown; so spread a kind word to all you see, because what you speak can make the difference in me. Go ahead and talk I say, for your words could very well make or break my day, but be aware, that your words have care, for the words you dare, you may have to bear.} Words are meaningful. [Word – (werd) n a meaningful sound which stands for and idea:] Meaningful- (SYN) profound, deep expressive, important crucial]

So before God spoke us into existence by His words; we were a profound and important idea, which brought forth a meaningful sound. So our mere existence was crucial to God.

Be careful of your words, for after whatever you've said; something will happen; things will form and things will change; just by (your) WORDS alone.

No weapon that is formed against thee shall prosper; and every TONGUE! (word) that shall rise against thee in judgment thou shalt condemn. This is the heritage of the servants of the Lord, and their righteousness is to me, saith the Lord Is. 54:17

A thought to Remember

W e've heard the old saying, that goes; "sticks and stones may break my bones, but words will never hurt me." But I say, "sticks and stones will break you bones and words will kill you." Be careful of the words you say to people, especially to children, Words are Powerful; for it was by words that the world was created. It was by words, we were created and it was words that was apart of my daughters death, negative words. Death and life are in the power of the tongue and they that love it shall eat the fruit thereof. [Prov. 18:21] What are you speaking with your tongue? Is it life or is it death? Is it good fruit or is it bad fruit? Thou are snared with the words of thy mouth; thou art taken with the words of thy mouth.

But he answered and said, it is written, man shall not live by bread alone, but by every word that proceedeth out of the mouth of God. [Matt. 4:4] Find out what God has said about you, concerning you and after you know what he said, then don't let no devil in hell or out make you think any differently than what your Father have spoken.

This is what he said about us; For I know the thoughts that I think towards you, saith the Lord, thoughts of peace and not evil, to give you an expected end. [Jer. 29:11] He also said, in Psalm 138:8 The Lord will perfect (finish) that which concerneth me: thou mercy, oh Lord, endureth forever: forsake not the works of thine own hands. What these scriptures are saying, is that God's thoughts and feelings toward us is of peace and prosperity and everything that we have a concern about he's going to see to it, that it is completed and brought to pass: because he will not forsake (us) the works of his hands. In the first chapter of the first book (Genesis) which means beginning, the words **"And God said"** are mentioned nine times. So, in the beginning of all life there was something **said;** and after every **said something** was formed and changed. In the beginning, during and after.

In your life and in the lives of others, what are you saying and what have you said. **WORDS!**

My A.T.A.M.
In Relationships

1. any time a man has a problem saying I love you
2. any time a man home boys don't know you're his girlfriend
3. any time a man gets money from you more than he gives to you
4. any time a man avoids the subject of the two of you
5. any time a man wants to be in control all the time
6. any time a man lets you do 90% of the calling
7. any time a man can't say you're my girlfriend/fiancé
8. any time a man wants to sleep with you before he say, I Do
9. any time a man stop calling and you don't hear from him in a while
10. any time a man say I'm not ready for marriage now, after dating 3 years
11. any time a man can hit you
12. any time a man mother feels he should marry his babies mom
13. any time a man uses profanity in your presence
14. any time a man let you get the door and he walk through first
15. any time a man can't treat you like a lady
16. any time a man blows cigarette smoke in your face
17. any time a man don't want to be seen holding your hands in public

18. any time a man ask what you want to get married for
19. any time a man can't tell you who just beeped or called
20. any time a man spends more time at his babies mama's house
21. any time a man avoids questions about his ex
22. any time a man has a problem with the men in your life (Dad, Brothers, Pastor,)
23. any time a man avoids the subject of his salvation
24. any time a man doesn't have a car, no money, no job, no place to live
25. any time a man forgets your birthday and other important dates
26. any time a man can't seem to do what you like or love
27. any time a man thinks marriage will mess up what you have now
28. any time a man says he's saved and you see no fruits
29. any time a man can't stay in service for the preached word
30. any time a man disrespects his mother or you
31. any time a man mother calls you just a friend
32. any time a man invites you and his ex to the same function
33. any time a man lets his ex eat from his plate in your presence
34. any time a man has low self esteem or he's insecure
35. any time a man has your car and can't come take you out or see you
36. any time a man looks guilty (smile)
37. any time a man can't stand up for you, choosing his mother over you
38. any time a man let's you pay the restaurant bill most of the time
39. any time a man wants to use your credit cards
40. any time a man doesn't know if he's in love with you
41. any time a man can't see where he's wrong and can't say I'm sorry
42. any time a man isn't interested in your goals and dreams
43. any time a man doesn't make you feel like his queen
44. any time a man can't help you to the next level of your ministry
45. any time a man isn't reaching out to you more than you are to him

46. any time a man can't be the spiritual leader of the house
47. any time a man can't respect you opinions
48. any time a man can't tell you the truth
49. any time a man isn't a man
50. any time a man can't respect your parents and their wishes
51. any time a man wants to pull you away from your family
52. any time a man won't hear nobody
53. any time a man can't control his temper
54. any time a man can't pay for the taxi
55. any time a man ask for your phone number and never call you
56. any time a man can't say I miss you too
57. any time a man tells you to buy a card for you from him
58. any time a man can't buy you a card
59. any time a man tells you your dinner isn't free
60. any time a man only call every other full moon

"When helping you is hurting me, when keeping you is killing me," these are just a few of the A. T. A. M. that I could think of, but I'm sure you can think of a few more. If so Please! First of all come to grips with the truth that your relationship needs help. Another thing, we can't change no one or make them the way we want them to be. Who they are, is what they will be. Only God can do the changing and make the difference. And men, these a.t.a.m. can be any time a woman.

So for the women who have husbands that are found wanting in some of these areas, if you checked a least five or more then the both of you need to have a serious and prayerful communication session. And for all of my single sisters (like me), if you have checked off even one from this entire list, then a red flag needs to go up; I'm serious. Life is to short too be playing with your life and even shorter if someone else is playing with it. To those that are 39 or over, if a young man come up to you trying to hit on you; ask him what are his intentions, his plans and if they are not long term plans **(MARRIAGE!!!),** then tell him to take a long slow ride to the devil's house. And then you need to know how much money he makes, in other words **does he have a JOB!!!** No, I'm not encouraging you to be a gold digger, as people may think, but if two people are planning to marry then you need to know how secure and stable your finances are and will be in the future. As the old saying goes, "if you fail to plan, then you plan to fail." Please! Take it from me.

No, we don't want anything to happen to us or our marriage, but if it does, you need to have a plan, I didn't.

Once you fall in love or think you're in love you ain't gone listen to nobody! I've been there and done that. So Please! Stop! Look! and Listen to the voice of Jesus: whether he speaks directly to you or through a person. LISTEN!!! Don't want to be loved so bad until you fall for anything and end up doing the wrong thing; I did.

My Statements of Love
Given by my best friend
5/11/02

I Believe love to be the only powerful force of all good deeds.

I Believe love to be the thread that goes from heart-heart, race-race, color or creed.

I Believe God is love and I was created in his image therefore, I am the image of love.

I Believe that love is a Spirit, so therefore I love unconditionally at all times.

I Believe that love is music. voices, instruments, hand claps and feet all working rhythmically together bringing joy to all that will hear.

I Believe that love is the air that keeps blood flowing to the heart, with the pulse beating give life.

I Believe that love can stand alone, but <u>two</u> is better than one. "What if <u>all</u> loved?"

I Believe that love is a huge canvas and we are the painters. What stroke of love will you leave when your turn comes?

I Believe that love is pure, understanding, truthful and honest at all times.

I Believe that love reaches beyond what I see and feel and helps me to deal with what I know.

I Believe that love is a mirror it only reflect what it sees or what's put before it.

I Believe that love forgives and love with time will heal.

About the Author

There is so much to say about shun; I really don't know where to start, but my mind goes back to many incidents that has happened in her life and I think about her as this unique, little quiet child, always sitting back, somewhere watching me and looking like she was expecting for something great to happen any moment. I noticed how much she would be paying close attention to what I would say; and Phyllis did something one day and I said, "Phyllis, where did you come from," and Shun looked up at me with her big beautiful brown eyes and said, "Mother, she must have come from Alabama, that's where she came from." But Shun, I am so glad that you had the courage, and the nerves to sit down and write this book. I believe that Shun's book is one of the greatest things, besides her singing and ministering that women and men all over the world will be inspired, encouraged and blessed by this book.

Shun is a special child, out of ten she's the fifth child and the fourth daughter, right there in the middle. Every day she would sit and watch the airplanes go by or sit in the window watching the red light blink on and off from the radio/TV tower. Not knowing that one day she would be flying through the air, busy and busy can be, going from one end of the world to the next; preaching singing and teaching the gospel. I'm very thankful that she got save at an early age and gave God her life. She was always serious about her salvation, she never played around or tried to cut corners. She was serious about her soul. Shun had a habit when she was a little girl (like most children) and I wondered so many times, how could I break this habit, because she was about to start school and I said, "Lord my baby is gonna start school, she sucks her thumb, she's gonna be picking up everything and touching things; all those germs! God, you've got go give me a way to stop Shun from sucking her thumb." I remember one day I had her on punishment and while she was sitting on the floor sucking her thumb, I said to myself, "I've tried everything; I put hot sauce on it, I've wrapped it and tied it up; I put tape on it, just everything, so I thought within my heart." Then I said , I'm gonna tell her that, if she really love Jesus, she'll stop sucking that thumb". So I said, "Shun! are you save?" she said, "yes ma'am", I said, "Shun if you really love Jesus like you act like you do, you wouldn't suck that thumb anymore." God gave me the answer and she stopped.

I didn't know that she would become this great and wonderful gospel singer, (you're tops to me). I love the C. Sisters, and God knows how much I love Pastor S. C. but to me you are number one. She use to sing to me every night before going to bed, our favorite song was, "Love lifted me, by Curtis Eugene Martin". Sometimes I would fall off to sleep fires and then at times she would. I enjoyed that dedication she had tome. She would ask, "Mother you want me to sing to you tonight?" And now you are grown, you got married, and had two beautiful daughters and God saw fit to take Xenia and he left you with one beautiful daughter. I yet love to hear her sing and she yet put me to sleep at night. I ride down the street with her playing in my car on the way to church. She just blesses me.

Shun, I want you to know that, you are a strong woman! You are very strong, because the things you went through, the devil designed it to take your mind; but the love that you have for God: "Hallelujah", the walk that you have with the Lord, I'm not saying she's perfect and that she never did anything wrong. Because when I stand in the mirror myself, I see an imperfect person; striving to be. And because we strive, the Lord helps us, keeping us going, strengthens us to do his will. We fall down, but we get up. This book is going to bless many, many thousands of people. This book is going to cause marriages to be mended and broken hearts to be mended too. I also want to say, that I like the way she put God first, regardless of what or who may come and go. I've seen her go through, "Lord have mercy", I've prayed many times; "God keep my daughter, keep her mind in the midst of what she's going through now. Here she go again, go to go back to court, ain't done nothing, but try to take care of children and be a blessing to others". This would happen again and again and again, it wasn't always easy, but her Daddy and I would pray; "God whatever she face today in court, will you please give her the victory; don't let this take her under" and God did just that. I'll never forget, one time in court, when God did the miraculous for her and she took time, went prostrate before the Lord and whoever could see. They saw her giving God thanks, for giving her the victory one more time. My pastor use to say, (which was a Sunday school topic) "that after every victory is another trial," and I've seen a lot of trials come in her life, but the victory also came. Shun, I want you to know I love you and I thank God for you. I pray that your daughter will grow up to be as strong in the Lord as you are and have faith in God, that if he said it, he'll bring it to pass. [God is not a man, that he should lie; neither it he son of man, that he should repent: hath he said it, and shall he not do it? or hath he spoken, and shall he not make it good? Num. 23:19]

But Shun, I want you to know you are some woman in the Lord and I thank God for you. I thank God for allowing me to be your Mother. I am blessed of the Lord for having nine beautiful daughters, one wonderful son, seven grand children, and one great grand and for having the most wonderful husband that God ever let live.

I am a blessed woman, and I'm so thankful; and so glad God allowed me to give birth to such an anointed vessel, to such a humble woman, who never like fussing or arguing. Always peaceful and easy to get along with, but don't mess with her about God; she will let you know where she stands and that blesses me. We can't let our mistakes take us under, because the bible says; greater is he that is within us, than he that is in the world. I remember a saying, growing up that said, "many things may entangle our feet, but none shall hold us fast", that mean, we may get into something, but God will always deliver us and bring us out. It's all about God! It's about God or nothing; and that's the way I see it. Shun, God's greatest blessings are yet waiting to over take you. You were taken advantage of, people taking your money, left you in a lot of debt, but you overcame every obstacle, it's a blessing to see you. When I look at you, "Uh! Glory to God" I see a miracle, a woman standing tall, with her head on right and up straight. I see a woman that has great ambition and great determination in her, but most of all in God. Thanks be to God who gave you the victory, because the worst is over, and the best is yet to come. I'll never forget those days when she went to work for me, came home and gave me the check, without taking a penny. She only said, "Mother I'm just glad that I can go for you". And she never brought it up in my face or anything. You can't find many daughters like that. She calls me 'Queen' and her daddy 'King'. But shun, you are the Queen. I thank God that your life has touched my life, you've inspired me in so many ways and you've been a encouragement to your sisters and to others around you. Just remember what Paul said, to be content in whatever state you're in. That's how I see you; nothing is too heavy to keep you from praising Him or Worshipping Him. I love that about you. I just thank God for you, may He bless you and keep you in the best of health, in his riches, his glory and his wealth. Shun belongs to God.

(Missy./ Evang) Mother Bettie Ann Pace
Mother of the Author